Women, Reason and Nature

Women, Reason and Nature

Some Philosophical Problems with Feminism

Carol McMillan

Princeton University Press
Princeton, New Jersey

To my mother and father

Contents

Acknowledgements

This book grew out of an M.Phil. thesis written at King's College, London. During the time that I was writing it I had many valuable discussions with Professor Peter Winch, who led me to explore new and exciting areas of study and for whose help, guidance and encouragement over the years I am deeply grateful.

Mr Rai Gaita and Professor D. Z. Phillips very kindly made many constructive criticisms of the original thesis and encouraged me to prepare it for publication. Mr Christopher Winch and Miss Marina Barabas also provided useful criticism of the original thesis. Mrs Marge Phillips kindly helped with the translation of Simmel's German text.

Special thanks are due to my family, my mother-in-law and my friend, Mrs Dibbie Jarvis. They all gave freely of their time and affection in helping to care for my two sons while I worked.

The final debt is a great one, owed to my husband, Mike, for his generous co-operation. Over the past four years he has done many of the necessary things I had no time for in order to allow me time to work and, through his criticism, has consistently helped me to get closer to what I really wanted to say. I do not know how to thank him.

The author and publisher would like to thank the following for permission to quote passages from their publications: Basil Blackwell Publisher: A. I. Melden, *Rights and Persons* (Oxford, 1977); Ludwig Wittgenstein, *The Blue and Brown Books* (Oxford, 1975) and *Philosophical Investigations* (Oxford, 1974). Cambridge University Press: Julia Annas, 'Mill and the Subjection of Women', *Philosophy*,

52, 1977; George Sturt, *The Wheelwright's Shop* (Cambridge, 1976). Jonathan Cape Ltd and Alfred A. Knopf, Inc.: Simone de Beauvoir, *The Second Sex*, trs. H. M. Parshley (London, 1953). Collins Publishers and Harper & Row, Publishers, Inc.: Malcolm Muggeridge, *Something Beautiful for God* (London, 1980). J. M. Dent & Sons: Jean-Jacques Rousseau, *Emile* (London, 1977). Faber and Faber Limited and Harcourt Brace Jovanovich, Inc.: T. S. Eliot, 'Choruses from "The Rock"', *Collected Poems 1909—1962* (London, 1972). Reprinted by permission of Faber and Faber Ltd/ copyright 1936 by Harcourt Brace Jovanovich, Inc.; copyright 1963, 1964 by T. S. Eliot. Reprinted by permission of the publisher. Fontana Paperbacks: Sheila Kitzinger, *Women as Mothers* (London, 1978); Fontana Paperbacks and the author: Rudolph Schaffer, *Mothering* (London, 1977). Victor Gollancz Ltd and William Morrow & Co., Inc.: Margaret Mead, *Male and Female* (London, 1950). Granada Publishing Ltd and Doubleday & Company, Inc.: Kate Millett, *Sexual Politics* (London, 1972). Copyright © 1969, 1970 by Kate Millett; reprinted by permission of Doubleday & Company, Inc. Heinemann and William Morrow & Co., Inc.: Danaë Brook, *Naturebirth* (London, 1976); Heinemann and Alfred A. Knopf, Inc.: Kahlil Gibran, *The Prophet* (London, 1970). Reprinted by permission of Alfred A. Knopf, Inc.; copyright 1923 by Kahlil Gibran and renewed 1951 by Administrators CTA of Kahlil Gibran Estate, and Mary G. Gibran. Hutchinson & Co. Ltd and Barnes & Noble Books: Immanuel Kant, 'Groundwork of the Metaphysics of Morals', trs. H. J. Paton, in *The Moral Law* (London, 1969). Oxford University Press: Leo Tolstoy, *The Kreutzer Sonata, The Devil and Other Tales* (London, 1973); William Wallace (trs.), *The Logic of Hegel* (Oxford, 1874); Simone Weil, *Selected Essays 1934—1943* (London, 1962). Penguin Books Ltd: Thomas Gladwin, 'Culture and Logical Process' from *Tinker, Tailor . . . The Myth of Cultural Deprivation*, ed. Nell Keddie (Harmondsworth, 1973), this selection copyright © Nell Keddie, 1973; Sheila Rowbotham, *Woman's Consciousness, Man's World* (Harmondsworth, 1973), copyright © Sheila Rowbotham 1973. Laurence Pollinger Limited and William Morrow & Co., Inc.: Shulamith Firestone, *The Dialectic of Sex* (Jonathan Cape Ltd, London, 1971). Putnam Publishing Group:

Carol Gould, 'The Woman Question: Philosophy of Liberation and the Liberation of Philosophy' from *Women and Philosophy,* ed. Carol Gould and Marx Wartofsky (New York, 1976). Routledge & Kegan Paul Ltd: Peter Winch, *Ethics and Action* (London, 1972); Routledge & Kegan Paul Ltd and the University of Massachusetts Press: Simone Weil, *Oppression and Liberty* (London, 1972). *Socialist Worker*: Valerie Clark, 'When Did You Last See Your Wife?' from *Socialist Worker,* 10 October 1970 (quoted by Sheila Rowbotham, *Woman's Consciousness, Man's World,* p. 93). University of Chicago Press: Hannah Arendt, *The Human Condition* (Chicago, 1974). Reprinted by permission of The University of Chicago Press. Viking Penguin Inc.: Hannah Arendt, 'The Crisis in Education' from *Between Past and Future: Eight Exercises in Political Thought* (New York, 1958). Copyright © 1958 by Hannah Arendt. Reprinted by permission of Viking Penguin Inc.

Introduction

Despite the diversity of the views of those who call themselves feminists, there is at least one view which is central to the thinking of them all. This is the notion that the process of moral argument presupposes the principle that everyone should be treated equally. This principle derives from the view that since the common respect due to all persons is based on the fact that they are rational beings, there is no moral justification for treating people differently because of their age, sex, intelligence or colour.

The thrust of feminist argument has therefore, for the most part, rested on the belief that since (apart from reproduction) there are no important differences between the sexes, nothing can justify a segregation of their roles. Any differences which may exist are said to be fostered culturally by forcing women to concentrate their activities exclusively in the domestic sphere. This in turn leads to the development of supposedly feminine traits such as self-sacrifice and passivity, which has the added consequence of inhibiting the development in women of their potential as rational, intellectual and creative beings. The argument that women be excluded from the public sphere because of an innate incapacity is thus shown to be incoherent; feminists conclude that women should be treated the same as men. Indeed, they emphasize that any attempts to educate the sexes differently are to be opposed strenuously, lest we find ourselves faced yet again with the sorts of social circumstances that prevent women from demonstrating their true capacity for reasoned activity. The feminist's moral, put quite simply, is this: confine women to the domestic sphere, make them fit primarily for looking after a husband and children, and you will be faced with a debased creature lacking in human dignity.

In this way, the assumption that reasoning is a characteristic peculiar only to those pursuits that have traditionally been confined to men — and that traditionally feminine roles such as child-rearing and home-making involve little or no use of the reasoning or intellectual faculty — is taken to be axiomatic on both sides of the debate between feminists and sexists. The attempt to justify all sorts of views about the inferiority of women by appealing to their lack of a deliberative faculty is thus seen by both feminists and sexists to be a reasonable one. Consequently, it seems that the crucial issue in the debate is the question of whether or not, given equal educational and occupational opportunities, women will in fact prove themselves in the world of 'reason'.

And yet, I shall argue, it is precisely the argument that feminists use — the distorting effects of a faulty education and upbringing — that both answers and bypasses the issues involved. This is because feminists share with their antagonists views about the nature of rationality and about the relation between reason and personhood that are plagued with difficulties.

1

Women and Reason

Some philosophers, particularly those associated with the Hegelian tradition in one way or another, have tried to argue that there are two different theories of knowledge for the human species, that there is a rational or *a priori* basis to the fact that certain pursuits are peculiarly masculine and others are peculiarly feminine, which can be justified by talk about masculine and feminine natures respectively. This point of view is advanced particularly well in Georg Simmel's essay 'Das Relative und das Absolute im Geschlechter-Problem'.

Simmel begins his essay with a criticism of the norms by which we judge the world and concludes that they are neither independent nor neutral, but reflect a particular standpoint. The tendency, therefore, to think of civilization as 'human' civilization is ill-founded, for if we look more closely, we shall see that this supposed human civilization is, in fact, male-dominated and in no way reflects the position and thoughts of that other half of mankind, woman. His argument rests, for the most part, on the Hegelian idea that art, general morality, social ideas and theoretical knowledge are all attempts by men to unite reality with the Idea, to transcend the subject—object dyad. And precisely because these pursuits are attempts to unite reality with the Idea, it is absurd to decry women for not being interested in them. His contention is that because people have failed to see that the condition of womanhood, unlike that of manhood, is actually to exist in a pre-dualistic state (or outside the subject—object dyad), the so-called lack of logic or reason in women, far from being a fault, is merely indicative of their comfortable existence in that unification of life and the Idea which

1

the male sex is still so desperately trying to achieve. This means that any attempt to persuade women to take an interest in art, morality, social ideas or philosophy can only be the result of crooked thinking.

How has this mistake been made? Simmel suggests that women are judged according to male rather than female norms because we fail to see that there is an asymmetry both in the empirical and in the metaphysical nature of the two sexes. As a result, all sorts of misunderstandings about women arise because judgements are made about them which are appropriate only to that other being, man. What Simmel does is to remind us that there are certain physical and metaphysical differences between the sexes which must be taken into account if this error is to be avoided in the future. By contrast, he argues that when we come to see the differences in the behaviour and activities of the sexes in the light of the *a priori* principle that only men are imprisoned in the subject—object dyad, many things that now strike us as enigmatic, mysterious or odd about women will no longer do so.

By way of example, he discusses the different sexual lives of men and women in the light of the above principle and draws attention to the nature of the asymmetry between them. He reminds us that a man's sexual life is experienced only in the act of copulation and thus exists for him, necessarily, in his relation to woman. A woman's sexual life cannot, by contrast, be so easily compartmentalized, separated from the rest of her life, since it is experienced not only in the act of copulation but also in the full reproductive cycle: menstruation, copulation, conception, parturition and lactation. This fact is significant for Simmel because it is a reflection of the metaphysical differences between the sexes, demonstrating that man exists in an extensive relation to the world, while woman exists in an intensive one — which is another way of saying that since man depends on something outside himself (namely, woman) for sexual gratification, his world lacks inner unity or harmony and is therefore based on the subject—object dyad, whereas in woman sexual harmony is supposed to be an expression of the fact that she relates to things through direct, instinctive contact. In other words, the fact that woman exists outside the subject—object dyad manifests itself in the harmony of her sexual life. Always there is this asymmetry between man and woman. Man reaches beyond himself, relates himself to a beyond that results in the splitting of the unity of life into the forms of subject/object, judge/judged, means/end, with which he aims to re-establish the unity he has lost; woman, on the other hand, is in a pre-dualistic stage.

This basic structure reveals, for Simmel, the tragedy of the sexes. The male sex created the productive relationship between being and the world but has always to come up against the finiteness of this activity, for man is severely limited by the constraints imposed upon him by the world. Woman's life, in turn, is made tragic simply by virtue of her relationship with man. Simmel maintains that the category means/end is rooted so deeply in man that he is capable of valuing woman only as a means of achieving certain ends — running the house, producing offspring and so on. But the fact that woman is not intended by nature to be a means-being is apparently revealed by the fact that constant hard work makes her ugly, which is not so in the case of man. Simmel further argues that the reason why woman is made unhappy by being an object of observation is because she has been reduced to a means. Equally, the reason why woman is passive is because a nature resting on an inner, relation-free subjectivity will inevitably play the passive role when it meets an extensively related, aggressive being. In short, the tragedy of woman is a result of the fact that she is set down in a world of 'others', unavoidable relationships with whom break through the peace and calm at her inner centre.

For Simmel, then, the fact that women are outside the subject—object dyad means that they have no use for reason or logic, and it is because of this, rather than for any historical or physiological reasons, that they are intuitive beings. This argument is connected fundamentally with his contention that only art, morality, theoretical knowledge and social ideas — the world of culture — depend on the use of reason, which in turn presupposes the formation of the subject—object dyad. Quite what this assertion amounts to, however, cannot be fully understood without turning to Hegel.

One point about which Hegel seems adamant is that the basis of knowledge cannot depend on 'immediate facts of consciousness', 'self-evident truths' or mere instinctive feelings (the then fashionable view of romanticism)[1] because such subjectivism would lead to an extreme form of relativism and to the denial of the possibility of knowledge. Troubled most by the problems of ethical relativism, Hegel emphasized that subjective thinking lacks any criterion for verification and makes it impossible for a person to make a rational choice between a variety of programmes. The authority of knowledge or of an ethical code cannot rest on a single individual's feelings or intuitions but must be grounded in the public realm of reason. It is only the state, argues Hegel, that can provide the universal element by which knowledge or morality is guarded against individual caprice. By wishing to place the individual before the state, subjectivism fails to see that only the state can express the universality present in public authority. The only guarantee against the natural tendency of subjectivism towards egoism, therefore, is the universal expression of the wishes of all members of the state. Thus even the family, for example, cannot provide a guard against egoism because it becomes an *égoisme à quatre, à cinq* and so on, which has to be transcended by that genuine universality which the individual achieves apparently only in so far as he is a true citizen, a member of the state.

To wish to return to a state of nature, therefore, is simply foolish, because for man knowledge is necessarily attained through the use of reason, through philosophy and deep reflection, rather than being acquired in the natural state which is peculiarly the sphere of animals. And, for the most part, Hegel's aim in philosophy seems to have been to publicize this fact. He wanted to demonstrate how necessary it is for the human spirit to individuate itself by full participation in the state and to give up its natural harmony with nature before it can achieve true unity with the Idea. Hence in his discussion of the Mosaic Legend of the Fall of Man in the *Logic*, he argues that the traditional interpretation, according to which it is assumed that man is punished because he is not intended to seek knowledge but ought to

[1] What Hegel has in mind is a false view of Rousseau, according to which it is claimed that the latter was arguing for a return to savagery. Accordingly, when I speak of romanticism, it is with specific reference to a position like that of Rousseau in *Emile*.

remain in a state of innocence, ignores the important fact that this would actually condemn him to being nothing more than an animal. Furthermore, since man's vocation is actually to strive to be in the image of God, knowledge is divine and far from being wrong and unnatural. Thus Hegel reminds us of God's words: 'Behold Adam is become as one of us, to know good and evil.' (*Logic*, p. 47) Consequently, he concludes:

The mind is not mere instinct: on the contrary, it essentially involves the tendency to reasoning and meditation. Childlike innocence no doubt has in it much that is sweet and attractive: but only because it reminds us of what the spirit must win for itself. The harmonious existence of childhood is a gift from the hand of nature: the second harmony must spring from the labour and culture of the spirit. And so the words of Christ, 'Except ye *become* as little children', etc., are very far from telling us that we must always remain children. (p. 46)

Accordingly, it is a mistake to regard natural and immediate harmony as the right state for man, for this must be given up before he can attain freedom. Thus

The prominent point in [the] curse is the contrast between man and nature. Man must work in the sweat of his brow: and woman bring forth in sorrow. Touching work, we remark that while it is the result of disunion, it is also victory over it. The beasts have nothing more to do but to pick up the materials required to satisfy their wants: man on the contrary can only satisfy his wants by transforming, and as it were originating the necessary means. (p. 47)

Hegel's point, then, is that since knowledge would lack objectivity and would depend on the caprice of a particular individual's feelings if it were based on intuition or on a natural harmony with nature, the precondition of knowledge is that man must give up the state of union with nature for that of the subject—object dyad. Hence the only possible reward for those who wish to go back to nature is not greater or finer knowledge but, as we saw earlier, a state comparable only with the life of animals.

It is important to note here that Hegel's argument is not so much against the individual's search for harmony or union with others, but rather against the view that this can be achieved by living on what he takes to be the merely natural, instinctive and subjective level of feelings. Indeed, his philosophy rests on the idea that 'unification pure and simple is the true content and aim of the individual, and the individual's destiny is the living of a universal life' (*Philosophy of Right*, p. 156). Nevertheless, human progress consists in moving further and further away from a peaceful harmony with nature and in achieving greater and greater differentiation until, by what looks like nothing more than mere sophistry on Hegel's part, the lack of unity becomes transcended and re-establishes its true and rational harmony in nothing less than the Hegelian system and the Prussian state.

We can see that Hegel wants to make every human accomplishment, whether it be in art, science, philosophy or morality, dependent on reason or on the subject—object dyad in order to emphasize the fact that, in contradiction to the dictates of romanticism, knowledge and the life of man (unlike that of animals) cannot be based on an intuitive union with nature. Like Kant before him, Hegel maintains, therefore, that what makes any feature of society peculiarly human is the fact that it is based on rationality and freedom rather than on the necessity of feelings and inclinations, and he deduces from this that the more ordered a person's life is, and the more it is lived according to strict principles and resolutions, the more ethical and human it will be. The upshot of this is that only those activities for which there is no counterpart in the animal world and which are not contaminated by feelings can be truly human and therefore based on reason.

Now, the view that what makes any activity specifically human is the fact that *absolutely no parallel for it exists in the animal world* is not peculiar only to Hegel but appears to have had, and still to have, considerable currency in our ways of thinking about the distinction between human beings and beasts. For example, such a view formed the fulcrum on which Greek political thought turned, as Hannah Arendt notes. She clarifies for us the distinction between the ancient

Greek idea of man as *zōon politikon* and the later idea of man as *animal socialis*, by emphasizing:

It is not that Plato or Aristotle was ignorant of, or unconcerned with, the fact that man cannot live outside the company of men, but they did not count this condition among the specifically human characteristics; on the contrary, it was something human life had in common with animal life, and for this reason alone it could not be fundamentally human. The natural, merely social companionship of the human species was considered to be a limitation imposed upon us by the needs of biological life, which are the same for the human animal as for other forms of animal life.

According to Greek thought, the human capacity for political organization is not only different from but stands in direct opposition to that natural association whose center is the home (*oikia*) and the family. (*The Human Condition*, p. 24)

Crucially, it is this way of thinking about the distinction between men and beasts, as much as anything, that is behind the feminist insistence that women must be liberated from the home. Carol Gould, for example, argues in 'The Woman Question':

The first mystification of woman as love goddess and madonna . . . is complemented by a second, equally pervasive mystification. Here the social and historical exploitation of women is hidden under the guise of its being her natural biological inheritance to bear and raise children, to be a housewife. This mystification seeks to keep woman in her place by making it her lot; it seeks to make her role acceptable by making it inevitable. Woman is regarded as by nature a childbreeder. In this way, woman is kept out of the public sphere, she is restrained from relating to other women and from becoming a public force, because she is understood as a creature not of discourse but of intercourse. This mystification treats woman as closer to animal than human nature. . . . That she is a natural rather than human being, and that she is a creature without a will, serves to rationalize using the woman as an instrument of production, as instrumental to the process of producing and reproducing the worker's life and that of future workers. . . .

Demystification, therefore, means a return from the 'heaven' of spiritualized femininity, and the 'hell' or ('jungle') of sheer animality to a changed social reality, in which the very basis for these mystifications is eliminated. (pp. 37—8)

Gould's contention is that much that can be described as distinctly human rather than animal activity has been unjustly reserved for men, whereas women have traditionally been confined to a domestic sphere, where the needs of biological life — for example, food, sex and procreation — which are the same for the human animal as for other forms of animal life, are provided for, thus denying women access to the public sphere. And if we add to this the fact that family relations are ordinarily based on inclinations and feelings of love and affection, it becomes clear why it is sometimes thought that women necessarily lie outside the realm of universal and rational principles on which the Kantian idea of duty is based.

Thus even Hegel, despite his rejection of the notion of intuitive knowledge, nevertheless maintains:

Women are capable of education, but they are not made for activities which demand a universal faculty such as the more advanced sciences, philosophy and certain forms of artistic production. . . . The difference between men and women is like that between animals and plants. Men correspond to animals, while women correspond to plants because their development is more placid and the principle that underlies it is the rather vague unity of feeling. When women hold the helm of government, the state is at once in jeopardy, because women regulate their actions not by the demands of universality but by arbitrary inclinations and opinions. Women are educated — who knows how? — as it were by breathing in ideas, by living rather than acquiring knowledge. The status of manhood, on the other hand, is attained only by the stress of thought and much technical exertion. (*Philosophy of Right*, pp. 263—4n.)

Curiously, the same philosopher who has been inveighing against the romantics, arguing that the basis of knowledge cannot be mere intuition or feelings but must involve differentiation and reason (see, in this instance, the Preface to the *Philosophy of Right*), wants to maintain, at the same time, that women live in the 'vague unity of feeling' and acquire knowledge through 'breathing in ideas'(!) when, even on his own terms, this is nonsense. For the sake of logic, he would have done better to conclude with Otto Weininger, a writer who follows Kant closely, that since women cannot properly be considered rational, they are therefore not really human:

Maternal love is an instinctive and natural impulse, and animals possess it in a degree as high as that of human beings. This alone is enough to show that it is not true love, that it is not of moral origin; for all morality proceeds from the intelligible character which animals, having no free will, do not possess. The ethical imperative can be heard only by a rational creature; there is no such thing as natural morality, for all morality must be self-conscious. . . .
  Maternal love, then, cannot be truly represented as resting on moral grounds. (*Sex and Character*, pp. 226, 225)

And if it is tempting to think that Weininger's view can be attributed to obnoxious male chauvinism, it is important to recognize that there is a persistent reverberation of his view in the feminist argument that it is the imposition on women of a specifically feminine role, conditioned at least in part by natural, biological facts, that has prevented them from exemplifying humanity at its best. A typical case is Kate Millett's complaint:

In terms of activity, sex role assigns domestic service and attendance upon infants to the female, the rest of human achievement, interest, and ambition to the male. The limited role allotted the female tends to arrest her at the level of biological experience. Therefore, nearly all that can be described as distinctly human rather than animal activity (in their own way animals also give birth and care for their young) is largely reserved for the male. (*Sexual Politics*, p. 26)[2]

[2] In her critique of Freud Millett herself points out that Freud's notion that women have not contributed, and for constitutional reasons cannot contribute, to civilization is based on the thought of Otto Weininger, 'a misogynist thinker to whom Freud was often indebted' (*Sexual Politics*, p. 188). However, she never seems to have come to terms with the philosophical reasons for this view and so fails to see, as I shall show, that there may be more in common between feminists on the one hand and rationalists like Freud and Weininger on the other than she would like to admit.

From this rationalist position, then, the fact that woman is engaged in many activities which have a counterpart in the animal world has made it difficult for philosophers both to admit that she is human and to say in what her humanity consists. Feminists have taken the obvious way out by arguing that if it could be shown that women are capable of achievement in those spheres that are more distinctly human (and traditionally male), then it would have to be admitted that they too are rational beings. Simmel's response, by contrast — for he too was dissatisfied with the implications of this argument — was to make out a case for showing that women are simply outside the subject—object dyad and, being more firmly rooted in the 'hidden and unknowable unity of life', are, in a certain sense, more fully human than men. Simmel's solution, however, cannot account for the facts.

We noted above, in connection with Hegel's discussion of the Mosaic Legend of the Fall, that the physical circumstances of human life — in which man must work in the sweat of his brow and woman must bring forth in sorrow — differing as they do from those of animal life, show that even at a fairly primitive level the relation of both man and woman with nature is one of opposition and discord. Hence the mere fact of necessity means that the human male is imprisoned in the subject—object dyad. Yet by Simmel's account and by Hegel's too the situation for woman is apparently otherwise. According to Simmel, the basic unity of woman's life means that there is never any opposition or conflict between her desires or her needs and those possible expedients that are open to her for satisfying them; moreover, since the harmony of her sexual life is an expression of the inner unity of her being, sex is more important to her than it is to man.

However, what he points to is only a specious harmony because although it is certainly true that sex for woman may involve conception, pregnancy, birth and suckling, as well as copulation, these, far from being the expression *par excellence* of peace, harmony and intuitive knowledge, are full of their own hardships, risks and dangers. There is nothing in a woman's life, just as there is nothing in a man's, that can shield her against possible calamity. She may be barren; she may suffer and die in childbirth; her children may be born in circumstances that are beset with poverty, misery and famine. A life without such misfortunes is just a grace of fate and not the *a priori* condition of the human female.

But there is something still more fundamentally wrong with Simmel's contention that any account of the importance of sex for women must rest on the idea that women do not reason or are outside the subject—object dyad. If it is true, as Schopenhauer once put it, that 'for women, only what is intuitive, present and immediately real truly exists; what is knowable only by means of concepts, what is remote, absent, past, or future cannot really be grasped by them' (*On the Basis of Morality*, p. 151), it is difficult to see how it is even intelligible to say that sex is important for them.

If a woman's sexual activity were restricted to certain quite definite periods and the role of copulation in her life were simply to allow for procreation (as in the case of animals), perhaps it might look as if we had something here that was pre-linguistic and pre-dualistic. If, with the onset of labour, a woman simply found a dark corner for herself in which to give birth (after the manner of a cat), there might be some room for talking of pristine unity. If the relation between mother and child were such that the dependence of a child on its mother were simply physical, there might be some room for talking as though the relation between mother and child were based on a sort of instinctual reflex.

But, of course, the issues of copulation, conception and nurturing in human females are not like that at all. The sexual life of women, and that of men too, takes place against a backcloth of values, of an intricately woven web of all sorts of beliefs, intentions, expectations and customs, to which no *a priori* limit can be set and which cannot be accounted for simply in biological terms. And this is something which shows itself both in the joy and in the suffering that a woman may experience from copulation and procreation:

Even now, when I do but remember my wife's life and the condition she was in during the first years when we had three or four children and she was absorbed in them, I am seized with horror! We led no life at all, but were in a state of constant danger, of escape from it, recurring danger, again followed by a desperate struggle and another escape — always as if we were on a sinking ship. . . . She herself suffered terribly, and continually tormented herself about the children and their health and illnesses. It was torture for her and for me too; and it was impossible for her not to suffer. After all, the attachment to her children, the animal need of feeding, caressing, and protecting them, was there as with most women, but there was not the lack of imagination and reason that there is in animals. A hen is not afraid of what may happen to her chick, does not know all the diseases that may befall it, and does not know all those remedies with which people imagine that they can save from illness and death. And for a hen her young are not a source of torment. She does for them what it is natural and pleasurable for her to do; her young ones are a pleasure to her. When a chick falls ill her duties are quite definite: she warms and feeds it. And doing this she knows that she is doing all that is necessary. If her chick dies she does not ask herself why it died, or where it has gone to; she cackles for a while, and then leaves off and goes on living as before. But for our unfortunate women, my wife among them, it was not so. (Tolstoy, *The Kreutzer Sonata,* pp. 158—9)

Reason, as the above description strikingly illustrates, is not a separate faculty operating in isolation from, and in contradistinction to, man's 'animal nature' — his feelings and his 'instinct' for food, sex and procreation — but shows itself in the character and the role that such needs may play in his life as a whole. And while it is true that man is fundamentally different from animal, there is something seriously misleading about the idea that reason is some sort of entity or faculty that is simply superimposed on his animal nature. For often the use of such terms as 'reason', 'intellectual faculty' or 'consciousness' to denote man's distinctiveness leads to talk not about real human beings but about disembodied, pure intelligence, so that reason becomes hypostatized as something existing by itself, outside any human activity or institution.[3] This is

---

[3] This view of the relation between rationality and human activities draws on Wittgenstein's account of the nature of meaning in his later philosophy, and particularly on the development of this conception in Peter Winch's *The Idea of a Social Science.*

what happens when Kant, for example, puts forward his conception of morality.

Moreover, this conception of man's nature may make us think of our needs as mere appetites, to be satiated with minimal fuss and maximal satisfaction. In our sexual relations we may forget that a relationship is something between two people and that the other is more than a mere *machine à plaisir*. For in sexual relations people are involved in ethical relations: obligations to the lover and possible further obligations in the event of a birth. It is because of this, and because of the complex emotions, intentions, thoughts and mores surrounding sex, that sex is something that matters to human beings. It is only against a certain background of values and traditions that it can make sense to imagine a man and a woman being concerned about the hollowness of, or the lack of deep satisfaction that they feel in, their sexual relationship, or to see why a person's sexual life can be characterized by feelings of guilt and revulsion or by extreme tenderness and strong passion. Ironically, it is the complex emotions and thoughts surrounding sex — those very features that make it nonsensical to suppose, despite the rationalist argument, that sexuality in human beings and animals (even female human beings) has anything other than a superficial similarity — that feminists are keen to exorcize from our behaviour and ways of thinking about sexual matters. For a world that happily tolerated 'free sexual expression' would also be a world in which sexuality would be merely one activity among others, like going for a walk or sleeping — as, indeed, is the case with animals.[4]

[4] See, for example, Mary Jane Sherfey, 'On the Nature of Female Sexuality'. Sherfey's thesis seems to be that the real nature of female sexuality can be more fully understood by focusing attention on the biological mechanism of the female erotogenic zones and by regarding sexual activity in the higher primates as a norm towards which to strive. Further, she thinks that people's sexual lives are healthier nowadays because modern sexuality is unconnected with the sorts of concern I have mentioned, notably 'a decided lifting of the ancient social injunctions against the free expression of female sexuality' (ibid., p. 152).

See also Shulamith Firestone, *The Dialectic of Sex*, p. 83.

Finally, for some pointed remarks against the idea that the chief characteristic of sexual problems is that they spring from inhibitions, see Rush Rhees, 'The Tree of Nebuchadnezzar' and 'Mario und der Zauberer'.

By the same token, the satisfaction of hunger is not the same for human beings as it is for animals. For animals it matters *only* that there should be enough to eat. For humans this matters too, although at times it may not matter at all: think of the Irish hunger strikers or religious fasts. The important point here is the distinctly human character of eating. How people prepare their food, how they serve it, which foods they find (morally or on religious grounds) acceptable or unacceptable, whether prayers of thanksgiving before meals are considered appropriate — all these are considerations that play a part only in *human* life.

A woman baking bread thus distinguishes herself from an animal as clearly as does a philosopher cogitating in isolation. For if we take note of the complicated surroundings in which most human activities occur, it is clear that there are few parallels with animal life. By tearing activities out of their contexts and by failing to see that it is the particular surroundings in which they occur that decide what sorts of description are appropriate, we assume, mistakenly, that those activities for which there is a parallel in the animal world are not distinctly human.

It can be seen, then, that if any explanation can be offered of why sex is important to women, it is that far from being a result of the fact that they do not reason, sex is important to them precisely because the animal state is not their natural one. Even in the domestic sphere the activities of women depend on foresight, preparation and training: this fact alone is enough to show how unwarranted are both the Hegelian restriction of rationality and knowledge to intellectual pursuits and the feminists' belief that if women are rational beings, then the domestic sphere cannot be their proper place.

Indeed, one reason why the whole issue of the humanity of women is problematic is precisely because it is assumed that human beings demonstrate their capacity for reason only in those activities which are absolutely distinct from those of animals; and, further, that those activities are always based on reason in the rationalist sense. Not only does this conception distort the nature of domestic activities, it also serves to falsify the nature of the numerous, traditionally masculine activities which do not fall neatly into this conceptual schema. To the extent that feminists feel compelled to argue that women should be equally placed in a man's world, their analysis is symptomatic of a false perception of the distinction between human beings and animals.

2

Reason and Emotion

Of course, it is true that those activities for which there is no parallel in the animal world do tend to be regarded with most respect and as mankind's highest achievements: we do indeed think of the world of culture (as opposed to the domestic realm) as the sphere in which mankind shows himself to be more than a mere animal. Men may not have wings, but they have made aeroplanes and spaceships to carry them through the air; men may die, but they sometimes remain immortal through artistic creation. And it is nevertheless true that women have remained, by and large, conspicuously absent from this sphere of achievement.

Feminists agree with their opponents that the achievements of the domestic sphere — if, indeed, traditional feminine activities like cooking and rearing children can be called achievements — are inferior. They argue, however, that women are largely absent from the history books not because they are incapable of great achievement, but because confinement to the trivial and petty life of the domestic, private realm makes it impossible for any human being to aspire to great originality and excellence. It is not women who are inferior, then, but the domestic realm, family life as opposed to the *polis*, where individuals meet and reveal their excellence.[1] Thus only when women are given access to the public world, allowed the possibilities of a career, can we reasonably expect any talent or genius among them to show itself. Moreover, it has been very convenient for men to enslave women in the home, subordinating

[1] This way of putting the distinction between the private and the public realm owes much to Hannah Arendt's discussion of the same. See chapter 2, 'The Public and the Private Realm', in *The Human Condition*.

them to the so-called needs of their children, for in this way they have presented no competition or threat to male dominance.

The idea that the private realm, the domain of family life, should be regarded as inherently inferior to the world of culture, even though the warmth of the hearth and the intimacy of family life are necessities for the healthy growth of human beings in the world, is a presumption very dear to sexists, which feminists themselves happily embrace. This presumption, however, if taken seriously, makes it impossible to see, for instance, why moral goodness, a virtue many sexists see as the exclusive property of men, should be thought a virtue at all.

According to a rationalist view like Hegel's, family life is inferior to that of the state because it is based on love. 'Love, however, is feeling, i.e., ethical life in the form of something natural. In the state, feeling disappears; there we are conscious of unity as law; there the content must be rational and known to us.' (*Philosophy of Right*, p. 261, addition to para. 158) This view echoes the idea that feelings are more evident in people who live close to nature and in animals because they are supposedly based on instincts or intuition. And since it is thought that feelings are always subjective and capricious, it follows that they cannot be the basis of morality until they become embodied in the state in the form of rational and universal principles. Feelings, and therefore family life which is based upon them, are inherently inferior, then, because they exist outside the realm of reason. Equally, in so far as morality is thought of as the zenith of human reason, love can have no place there. What is crucial here is not so much the view that family life is inferior as the thesis that feelings and love cannot be indicative of judgement and knowledge and the corollary to this, that morality must be independent of affection.

Now, rationalist ethics tends to think of goodness as the triumph of reason over inclination or feelings. This position is based partly on a certain view of the nature of a moral difficulty. It is argued that what makes a situation morally difficult is the tension that exists between doing what we *want* and what we *ought*. What we want seems so often to serve an egotistical desire that it must be assumed that we can be sure of acting morally only when our actions do not spring from natural inclination. Consequently, to argue that people should follow their innermost feelings, as the romantic is prone to do, is tantamount to asserting that a good society would be one in which individuals were actually encouraged to pursue their own interests with impunity. It is with this sort of issue in mind that Hegel comes down so heavily against romanticism, the view, as he puts it in the Preface to the *Philosophy of Right*, that 'that only is true which each individual allows to rise out of his heart, emotion, and inspiration about ethical institutions' (p. 5). For, according to this view, the possibility that our innermost desires may tempt us to do evil is never considered. But, more crucially, it leads to an extreme form of ethical relativism and, ultimately, to moral scepticism. In so far as this is a true characterization of romanticism, I think Hegel is right. Once an individual becomes answerable only to himself for his actions and feelings, without recourse to some public, external authority, the whole notion of ethics — the distinction between good and evil — collapses.

That is to say, no morality can exist outside the ethical sphere, for concepts such as good and evil are not defined by particular individuals; they are given meaning only by the form of life or the moral practices in which they operate.[2] It is not the individual who is the measure of what is good, Hegel would have argued, but the community. Morality as a social institution — in the sense of a body of ethical rules — has logical priority over the individual. Men are not self-contained atoms, each complete in itself. Consequently, to explain how a human being feels, thinks or behaves, we need to take account of something more than the human being himself. We need to call on the notion of a continuing society of such beings, each of whom participates in a common life. Without a common life, individuals — let alone moral individuals — would be unthinkable, since it is from society that people derive their most fundamental

---

[2] This view of moral practices and their justification follows the conception of D. Z. Phillips and H. O. Mounce in *Moral Practices*.

ways of thinking and acting. Human activities presuppose a social setting, and it is the rules of ethical grammar that provide the framework within which particular moral judgements are intelligible; therefore the idea of a moral agent making meaningful moral judgements in total isolation from such rules is unintelligible.

However, writers like Hegel have wanted to go further. In their zeal to point out that extreme ethical relativism is an inevitable consequence of wanting to give complete primacy to the individual, they fail to see that there is, nevertheless, a fundamental sense in which the individual may indeed be the final judge of what to do. This is so particularly when someone is faced with a moral dilemma.

The case to be considered is that of a person who accepts that ethical institutions, or the rules of ethical grammar, provide the framework within which particular moral judgements are intelligible. He concedes that the existence of unconditionally accepted moral principles is the precondition for the expression of moral judgements. Now he finds himself in a situation in which one moral principle can be upheld only at the expense of another equally fundamental principle and so is perplexed and bewildered about what he should do. For example, in Tolstoy's *Anna Karenina* Anna is faced with a terrible conflict. On the one hand, she can bring to an end a relationship with Karenin that has been based on falsehood and deceit; on the other hand, a new life with her lover, Vronsky, would mean that she would be severed from her child. She decides on the latter course of action.

Now, it could be argued that she ought to have chosen differently, that whatever the cost to her personal life, she should have stayed with her son and given up Vronsky. But that would be to miss the extent of her difficulty, for, as Tolstoy makes clear, however she acts, she will be involved in the betrayal of someone. The point is that in this sort of situation the final decision about how to act must rest with the person facing the difficulty. Anna must decide for herself how to act because there is no straightforwardly obvious, 'right' way. In such circumstances moral principles — no matter how public and objective the standards on which they are based may be — cannot offer her a firm guide to action. Indeed, it is because of the moral principles at stake — because of her commitment to her son *and* because of her refusal to participate any longer in a life based on dishonesty — that she is faced with this dilemma.

Thus while there is a superficial, and somewhat dangerous, sense in which the individual is the final arbiter of values, capable of willing anything, nevertheless his perception of a situation can be seen to be unique and unquestionable. It is this latter point that is too often forgotten in the arguments of the rationalists. For while Anna acts without the justification of any set of circumscribed rules — it might be true to say that in so acting she is trying to follow her innermost feelings — it would certainly be unjust to charge her with caprice.

Moreover, according to a rationalist account, it might be admitted that 'reason' has in fact failed to provide a solution here. But does it necessarily follow that a person in this awful situation has 'failed', that he or she has fallen from the lofty heights of a human and rational being to an animal-like state of chaos? Surely not: for the sufferings of men, no less than their triumphs, belong to a world that is essentially human and offer opportunities for gaining knowledge and wisdom. A refusal to grant that action based on natural inclination may sometimes be a legitimate way of responding to a moral difficulty obscures not only the nature of a moral difficulty but also the nature of goodness.

We have already noted that one reason why some philosophers wish to reject feelings as an appropriate basis for moral action is that their intrusion jeopardizes ethics. The problem, as I stated it earlier, can be put thus: how can we be sure that what we want is what we ought to want?

Kant goes so far as to say that no action springing from natural inclination can have moral worth. For him, an action has genuine moral worth only when it is done solely out of duty, without any liking or preference for it:

Suppose then that the mind of [a] man were overclouded by sorrows of his own which extinguished all sympathy with the fate of others, but that he still had power to help those in distress, though no longer stirred by the need of others because sufficiently occupied with his own; and suppose that, when no longer moved by any inclination, he tears himself out of this deadly insensibility and does the action without any inclination, for the sake of duty alone; then for the first time his action has its genuine moral worth. Still further: if nature had implanted little sympathy in this or that man's heart; if . . . he were cold in temperament and indifferent to the sufferings of others . . . if such a man (who would in truth not be the worst product of nature) were not exactly fashioned by her to be a philanthropist, would he not still find in himself a source from which he might draw a worth far higher than any that a good-natured temperament can have? Assuredly he would . . . namely, that he does good, not from inclination, but from duty. (*Groundwork of the Metaphysic of Morals*, p. 64)

Hegel is reiterating the same point when he says, as we saw above (see p. 17), that ethical life must be based not on love but on law, that an attempt must be made to find an absolute criterion according to which it can always be shown that particular sorts of acts are necessarily egotistical ones.

But while it is true to say that some acts that spring from natural inclination have no moral worth, it does not follow that all such acts must be morally worthless. The possibility that some may have moral value is ruled out *a priori* by rationalists because, at least in part, it is thought that there is a straightforward opposition between reasons and emotions, between the world of culture and the private realm of the family, between principled actions and spontaneous gestures or acts based on love, as a result of which the former category is always considered inherently superior to the latter one. To understand the reasons for such argument is to see what underlies the view that because women are thought to be emotional, they cannot therefore be capable of genuine goodness.

In fact, as Schopenhauer scathingly points out in *On the Basis of Morality*, the Kantian assertion that only those acts based on duty are good is an outrage to genuine moral feeling, the very opposite of the Christian doctrine of morals, which puts love before everything and teaches that without charity nothing profiteth. In opposition to

Kant, he reasserts that lovingkindness, or philanthropy, is the cardinal virtue of morality and has nothing to do with 'pitiful, miserable duty' because a man who helps someone in distress does so less because it is his duty than because someone who is in pain and is suffering *needs* help. The duty we have to others in such situations cannot be understood if we are incapable of feeling sympathetic towards their sorrows. Similarly, we cannot respond to their needs if we are preoccupied with our own because, it might be added, only those acts which are genuinely selfless can be expressive of loving-kindness.[3]

Moreover, how far removed Kant's man motivated by duty alone is from goodness becomes all the clearer in the light of the following conversation with Mother Teresa of Calcutta, recorded in Malcolm Muggeridge's book *Something Beautiful for God*:

Mother Teresa: . . . the spirit of our society [is] . . . total surrender, loving trust and cheerfulness. We must be able to radiate the joy of Christ, express it in our actions. If our actions are just useful actions that give joy to the people, our poor people would never be able to rise up to the call which we want them to hear. . . . We want to make them feel that they are loved. If we went to them with a sad face, we would only make them much more depressed.

Malcolm Muggeridge: Even though you took them things they needed.

Mother Teresa: It is not very often things they need. What they need much more is what we offer them. In these twenty years of work amongst the people, I have come more and more to realize that it is being unwanted that is the worst disease that any human being can ever experience. . . . For all kinds of diseases there are medicines and cures. But for being unwanted, except there are willing hands to serve and there's a loving heart to love, I don't think this terrible disease can ever be cured. . . . This is what we are aiming at, to bring to the people the willing hands to serve and the hearts to go on loving them. (pp. 98–9)

Mother Teresa's comments show that acts based on the Kantian

---

[3] For a penetrating discussion of the relation between self-love and evil, see Philip Leon, *The Ethics of Power*.

sense of duty would be sterile and fruitless, would fail to serve the needs of those whom she is trying to help. Yet according to Kant's account, we should be forced to accept the preposterous conclusion that in order to give their actions moral worth, Mother Teresa and her Sisters of Charity would have to greet their people poker-faced, presumably hating every minute of the life to which they have committed themselves. It was this conclusion that Schopenhauer rightly and angrily rejected. And, interestingly, notwithstanding his misogynistic tendencies, he happily admits that women are superior to men in goodness because 'they surpass men in the virtue of *philanthropy* or lovingkindness, for the origin of this is in most cases *intuitive* and therefore appeals directly to compassion, to which women are decidedly more easily susceptible.' (*On the Basis of Morality*, p. 151)

Precisely to the extent, then, that Schopenhauer abhorred the deprecation of feeling and compassion by the 'idolaters of reason', Kant and Hegel, he, of all people, was able to find nothing jejune in the idea that women not only are capable of moral goodness but actually excel in this respect. My suggestion is that the contrast in the attitude to reason of a philosopher like Schopenhauer on the one hand and of those like Kant, Hegel and Weininger on the other shows that much unashamed prejudice against women may have been based not so much on male pride or on a lust for power as on a philosophical conception of the distinction between human beings and animals, between reason and emotions, which made it extremely difficult to see how the apparent stupidity of women could be due to anything but the fact that they were less than human.

Yet so pervasive is the assumption that feelings are antithetical to reason that even Schopenhauer — despite his vehement hatred of the venerators of reason — believes that women excel at loving-kindness only because they do not reason and live on the level of subjective intuitions (see above, p. 11) — even though elsewhere he argues that what distinguishes human beings from beasts is the faculty of reason, that is

the capacity for universal, abstract, non-intuitive representations, called *concepts*, which are indicated and fixed by means of words. It is this faculty alone that actually gives man the advantage over the animal. For these abstract representations or concepts, in other words, *comprehensive summaries* (*Inbegriffe*) of many separate things, are the condition of *language*, and thereby of actual *thinking*. Again, by means of thinking they condition the consciousness not merely of the present, which the animals also have, but of the past and future as such. (ibid., p. 81)

This, he states, is one reason why animals have no conscious morality, a point, however, which paradoxically makes women both nothing more than animals and, at the same time, peculiarly capable of the cardinal virtue of morality, namely lovingkindness.

In short, Schopenhauer rightly sees that the rationalist emphasis on reason (in opposition to feeling) as *the* defining feature of the world of culture makes it impossible to recognize genuine moral goodness for what it is. Yet he proceeds according to his conception of feelings and compassion as nothing more than savage instincts deaf to the voice of reason: hence his contradictory view of women. He needs to see that feelings, like thoughts, have a cognitive aspect too. It is to this last point that we now turn.

In Dostoyevsky's *Crime and Punishment* Sonia urges Raskolnikov to confess his crime despite the likely consequences of this for their future life together. There is no hint or suggestion that they should run away or that Raskolnikov should try to keep the crime a secret — Sonia's only concern is that Raskolnikov should be happy, the condition for which being that in repenting and being punished, he will be expiated of his guilt. Her feeling towards the murderer is one of deep compassion. The magnanimity of that compassion shows itself in the fact that even though Raskolnikov neither reciprocates her kindness nor shows any immediate gratitude for it, she remains unshaken in her feelings.

It might be argued by those who distrust human emotions that if Sonia had not loved Raskolnikov, she would have seen to it that he was tried and sentenced immediately. Certainly, she would not have risked waiting to see whether he gave himself up. And this, the rationalist would argue, is precisely the trouble with love, particularly familial love: it is egotistical and selfish. The rational man, unaffected by emotion, would presumably report the crime immediately and see to it that justice is exercised.[4]

But this criticism misunderstands what is involved here. There is great tension in the book between the psychological and practical pressures on Raskolnikov to give himself up: the intolerable burden of living with such a secret and, finally, the profoundly disturbing realization that he is guilty of having committed a heinous crime and not merely of having rid the world of a mean and despicable old woman. What makes it impossible for Sonia to report the crime herself is the fact that Raskolnikov is the one who has committed it. Only *he* can confess, and he can confess only when he feels genuinely repentant. This is crucial because Sonia's fundamental concern is

---

[4] This position is typified by the following stricture Weininger offers on maternal love:

> Maternal love . . . cannot be truly represented as resting on moral grounds. . . . In the love of a man for a woman, or between persons of the same sex, there is always some reference to the personal qualities of the individual; a mother's love extends itself indifferently to anything she has borne. It destroys the moral conception if we realize that the love of a mother for her child remains the same whether the child becomes a saint or a sinner, a king or a beggar, an angel or a fiend. Precisely the same conclusion will be reached from reflecting how children think they have a claim on their mother's love simply because she is their mother. Maternal love is non-moral because it has no relation to the individuality of the being on which it is bestowed, and there can be an ethical relation only between two individualities. (*Sex and Character*, p. 225)

Weininger rightly sees that it is crucial to the notion of maternal love that a mother's love extends unconditionally to all her children. He fails to observe, however, that this emotion does not prevent her from recognizing their separate individualities. Authentic maternal love shows itself through pleasure at one child's successes and sadness at another's failings. Weininger seems to imply that the only way one can recognize a sinner (say) as an individual is to condemn him or disown him outright. But while that may be one response, it is important to realize that another is possible. A mother may be acutely aware of her son's wrongdoing and may therefore be moved to feel both shame on the one hand and pity and compassion for him on the other. She would not feel pity for him if he were a saint; she would feel something else. This shows that she can be keenly conscious of the differences between her children and still feel a tender love for them all, although in one case it may move her to sorrow and compassion and in another to happiness and joy.

with the suffering that the horror of having committed such a crime must be causing Raskolnikov: 'Oh, I don't think there's anyone in the world more unhappy than you are!' she says to him. From this perspective, the whole point about confessing, about being punished and being sent to prison, is that through penitential suffering Raskolnikov may be redeemed.[5] For if Raskolnikov were discovered and sent to Siberia but felt no remorse for his crime, on Sonia's account nothing would have been gained. This is why it would be pointless for *her* to report the crime.

The distinction to which I am trying to draw attention may become clearer by considering the following remarks of Simone Weil, in which she emphasizes the modern inability to understand the meaning of retributive justice:

The art of punishing is the art of awakening in a criminal, by pain or even death, the desire for pure good.

But we have lost all idea of what punishment is. We are not aware that its purpose is to procure good for a man. For us it stops short with the infliction of harm. That is why there is one, and only one, thing in modern society more hideous than crime — namely, repressive justice. . . .

All talk of chastisement, punishment, retribution, or punitive justice nowadays always refers solely to the basest kind of revenge. ('Human Personality', pp. 31—2)

And that is why, it might be added, Raskolnikov is so astonished that despite her obvious love for him, Sonia insists that he should publicly declare himself a murderer and go to prison.

'What are you to do?' she cried, suddenly jumping to her feet and her

---

[5] See Simone Weil's remark: 'In the life of the individual, the innocent must always suffer for the guilty; because punishment is expiation only if it is preceded by repentance. The penitent, having become innocent, suffers for the guilty, whom the repentance has abolished.' (*First and Last Notebooks*, pp. 115—16)

For further elucidation of the relation between guilt, repentance, punishment and expiation that I am assuming, see Peter Winch, 'Ethical Reward and Punishment', chapter 11 in *Ethics and Action*, and Michael Weston, *Morality and the Self*.

eyes, which had till then been full of tears, flashed fire. 'Get up!' She seized him by the shoulder, and he raised himself, looking at her almost in astonishment. 'Go at once, this very minute, and stand at the crossroads, bow down to all the four corners of the world — and say to all men aloud, I am a murderer! Then God will send you life again. . . .'

'. . . Is it penal servitude you're thinking of, Sonia? Do you want me to give myself up?' he asked gloomily.

'Accept suffering and be redeemed by it — that's what you must do!' (*Crime and Punishment*, pp. 433—4)

In other words, Sonia's behaviour seems paradoxical only because Raskolnikov is blind to the fact that what she seeks is the exercise not of repressive justice but of penitential punishment.

Seen against considerations of this sort — against a particular conception of the relation between remorse and suffering, expiation and punishment — Sonia's compassion for Raskolnikov is indicative not of selfish egoism but of moral wisdom. This view cannot be justified simply by saying that her action is based on a *feeling*: after all, she might just as naturally have loathed Raskolnikov for his crime. No: we are struck by her perception of what sorts of issues are at stake here and the essential role these cognitions play in the feelings she has for Raskolnikov. Moreover, the fact that her actions are not egoistic shows itself in her relation with life and other people and in her deprecatory attitude to herself. Her compassion is embedded in a particular situation, and it is that situation which reveals the true nature of her moral stance.[6] Given different surroundings and different cognitions, her feelings could instead be expressive of contempt or any number of other emotions. One has only to think of the contrast between Sonia's attitude to Raskolnikov

[6] Cf. Wittgenstein, *Philosophical Investigations*, para. 337: 'An intention is embedded in its situation, in human customs and institutions.'

See also Mark Fisher in 'Reason, Emotion and Love', who rightly asserts:

To show that a being which experiences emotions while never thinking, judging, wondering, believing, inferring, understanding, explaining, predicting is a being of which no coherent conception can be formed, is not difficult. The essential point is that emotions have intentional objects, objects whose existence depends upon belief.

and that of the convicts in the prison to see that feelings themselves admit of many possibilities.

In forcing a wedge between reason and emotion, rationalist writers like Hegel fail to see that what makes bodily states and sensations emotional is the presence of evaluations or cognitions. Although feelings involve bodily processes, they are nevertheless distinguishable from them. Emotions are appraised as reasonable or unreasonable, justified or unjustified. We distinguish between emotions like shame and embarrassment, sentimentality and love, by reference to the way in which the subject perceives the object of the emotion and to the surroundings in which the emotion is felt and expressed. Thus to contrast thought and emotion by assuming that the latter is devoid of all cognition is to miss one of its crucial features. This means, for instance, that if we were to judge Sonia's response to Raskolnikov's confession adversely, the criticism would turn not on the fact that she responds *emotionally* but on her perception of what sorts of issues are at stake and on the inappropriateness, therefore, of the emotion in question.

The upshot of this is that even if the contention that women are emotional or more susceptible to compassion than men are is actually true, it does not prove that they do not reason but live on an animal-like level of subjective intuitions. And the corollary to this is that the desire to make lovingkindness a cardinal virtue of morality, as Schopenhauer wishes to, need not mean that one is asking for a return to savagery. What it does mean is that the rationalist attempt to construe morality as a peculiarly masculine achievement, as one that depends on the subject—object dyad and on the suppression of feelings, is tantamount to the assertion that what we normally call goodness is something of which men must logically be incapable.

At any rate, to think that feelings are important and have their place only in a human life is not to commit oneself to a denial of objectivity and of the possibility of knowledge because, as we saw above, the notion of objectivity need not be restricted to those activities which are independent of feelings and emotions. Indeed, it must not be so limited if some of the most profound experiences and thoughts of men and women are to be recognized for what they are.

In effect, it shows that the rationalist account of knowledge cannot even accommodate those spheres of activity which rationalists would like to see as their special achievements because logic and rationality exist neither in any one thing nor in isolation from the diverse and concrete situations in which they have their place.

We can now see why to quarrel with the views of Hegel and Simmel about the rationality of women is to quarrel with their whole way of thinking about reason and logic. Simmel, to be fair, does strive to resist prejudice and rightly seems to have realized that there is something amiss in judging everything from the masculine point of view. However, by failing to see that emotion has its cognitive and rational aspects and that 'feminine' activities are subject to criticism and appraisal no less than masculine ones, he raises the status of femininity only at the expense of ultimately making a virtue of irrationality.

3

Reason and Intuitive Knowledge

The notion that women are emotional beings tends to go hand in hand with the view that they relate to the world on an intuitive level. This conception is used to justify the view that women are incapable of pursuing the same tasks as men, and a neat demarcation is thus made between the private and the public realm. However, we have just seen how, by aiming to exclude from the public sphere those actions that are based on natural inclination or on emotions, rationalists fail to account satisfactorily for the moral content of an act. I want to suggest, further, that the difficulties we encounter in trying to understand the nature of goodness under this schema are merely symptomatic of the fallacy that lies behind the attempt to give a general account of the distinction between the private and the public realm in terms of a strict contrast between reason and emotion, between rational and intuitive knowledge.

Hegel's criticisms of intuitive knowledge are based on the conviction that for man the attainment of knowledge is necessarily achieved through the use of reason or the subject—object dyad, through philosophy and critical reflection, rather than by virtue of the natural state which is peculiarly the sphere of animals. The human spirit must differentiate itself, therefore, and must give up instinctive harmony with nature before it can achieve true unity with the Idea. That is why Simmel thinks that intuitive knowledge is always pre-reason and that experiences of inner unity must be restricted to women precisely because they do not reason.

But this view points to a further difficulty with the Hegelian emphasis on differentiation, for it is wrong to assume that because someone has experience of inner unity and fulfilment, he or she necessarily neither thinks nor reasons. Simmel assumes this because

wrens ↓ = You can have feelings that are based on morals.

he follows Hegel in thinking that feelings are based on instinct and
are not at all related to a person's thoughts, beliefs and actions.

It may be that Simmel's conception of the inner unity of a
woman's sexual life is something like that scene described by
D. H. Lawrence in *The Rainbow*, when Anna, consumed with
ecstasy over her pregnancy, feels within herself a tremendous surge
of power and delight that is invulnerable to any intrusion from her
husband. But significant and deep though this experience of
pregnancy may be in a woman's life, it cannot be used to argue that
she is, at bottom, in a fusion of inner unity.

It is therefore no surprise that in the same chapter, 'Anna Victrix',
Lawrence also depicts how, at times, the honeymooning couple are
united in a marvellous rapture of sexual communion and how, at
other times, this gives way to naked aggression that springs from
conflict and selfishness. There is nothing exclusive about these two
states, and it is important to recognize that they may continually
give way to one another. Thus Lawrence's point would seem to be
that pure, consummated sex is an expression (or the reward, perhaps)
of the ability or readiness to lose oneself, of the suspension of
egotistical concerns.

There is therefore no guarantee, either for women or for men,
that their relationships will always be fulfilling. Indeed, even
suffering can take on a positive aspect in certain circumstances, a
possibility which would be ruled out by Simmel's insistence that the
inner unity of a woman's life is somehow demonstrated by the fact
that she is independent of necessity:

It was bad enough. But to her it was never deathly. Even the fierce,
tearing pain was exhilarating. She screamed and suffered, but was all
the time curiously alive and vital. She felt so powerfully alive and in the
hands of such a masterly force of life, that her bottom-most feeling was
one of exhilaration. . . . (*The Rainbow*, p. 192)

And, of course, this feeling of exhilaration does not last for ever.
This suggests further that it is absurd to think, as Simmel does, that
women do not reason and live only on the level of instinctive feeling.

Besides, there is nothing absolutely 'natural' about experiencing labour as Anna does; rather, the experience is internally related to the role that suffering and birth play in her life as a whole, to the kind of person she is and to all sorts of other contingencies in her life. Consequently, it is possible to describe quite different circumstances or ways of thinking about birth and suffering (say); by contrast, it is quite intelligible for a woman to say, as in the Newsons' book *Patterns of Infant Care in an Urban Community*: 'As far as I'm concerned, they can give me all the anaesthetic they've got. I just don't want to know anything about it, I think all that stuff about the joy of birth is a lot of nonsense.' (p. 27) Hence Simmel's idea that it is possible to decide, *a priori*, what role sex can play in a woman's life fails to take account of the fact that sex does not exist in isolation but is invariably tied up with all sorts of other features of her life and of the society in which she lives. If we want to understand how such different responses to labour are possible, we shall have to come to terms with two very different ways of looking at life. Still, the important point for the moment is that even if a woman does experience joy in labour, this does not preclude the fact that she does not live merely on the level of instinct. Given the appropriate context, such experiences are moments which may be cherished when they are recognized for what they are.

Just as it is possible to give examples of moments of peace and fulfilment in a person's life without denying that he or she is capable of reason, so it is possible to make sense of the notion of intuitive knowledge without resorting to ideas about magical powers or lapsing into subjectivism. The Hegelian emphasis on differentiation, coupled with the Kantian emphasis on reason as opposed to feeling, far from guaranteeing the objective status of knowledge, serves only to obfuscate the fact that there are important differences even between the 'rational' and 'masculine' pursuits of mathematics, art, philosophy, law and so on. For instance, the differences in the methods used by scientists and artists are not just incidental to the general pursuit of unifying life with the Idea,[1] but they say something about

---

[1] Some feminists also mistakenly believe that different activities have the same

the very different problems and projects with which scientists and artists are concerned. Equally, what makes us think of scientific discovery as a great achievement of the human mind may have little or nothing to do with why we think of art as such.[2] One can only learn what (say) mathematics is by looking at what mathematicians do. And the fact that a particular discipline cannot and does not aim at formulating rational and universal principles or laws ought to remind us that what counts as knowledge can differ remarkably from practice to practice.[3]

Probably because of the success of science, it is commonly assumed by philosophers that working according to strict principles and rules

---

ultimate goal. Shulamith Firestone, for example, writes:

> Culture . . . is the sum of, and the dynamic between, the two modes through which the mind attempts to transcend the limitations and contingencies of reality. These two types of cultural responses entail different methods to achieve the same end, the realization of the conceivable in the possible. In the first, the individual denies the limitations of the given reality by escaping from it altogether, to define, create, his own possible. . . . This search for the ideal, realized by means of an artificial medium, we shall call the Aesthetic Mode. . . .
>
> [The second] is the attempt by man to master nature through the complete understanding of its mechanics. The coaxing of reality to conform with man's conceptual ideal, through the application of information extrapolated from itself, we shall call the Technological Mode. (*The Dialectic of Sex*, pp. 164—5)

[2] Poetry is not a civilizer, rather the reverse, for great poetry appeals to the most primitive instincts. It is not necessarily a moralizer; it does not necessarily improve one's character; it does not even teach good manners. It is a beautiful work of nature, like an eagle or a high sunrise. You owe it no duty. If you like it, listen to it; if not, let it alone. (Jeffers 'Poetry and Survival', quoted by Rhees, *Without Answers*)

But the same could not be said about a scientific discovery. For us, a scientific discovery is important because of the control it enables us to have over nature. It is not that art or poetry is not very good at achieving this; the point is that this is irrelevant and outside the concerns of someone writing a poem, say. For further discussion of these issues, see Rush Rhees, 'A Scientific Age', *Without Answers*, pp. 1—13.

[3] Wittgenstein's discussion of the difference between a calculation and an experiment is a case in point; see his *Remarks on the Foundations of Mathematics*.

which can always be universalized is essential to the acquisition of knowledge. To use one's reason is to formulate a body of principles that is independent of, and yet common to, every human activity. One shows that one *knows* something by being able to subsume the important points in a neat system of laws. The difficulty of a particular task or the degree of skill or knowledge required to complete it thus become related to the degree of sophistication of the theoretical tenets on which it is based. If one cannot systematize one's insights, either one is considered incapable or non-rational or, if one's skills are really exceptional, it is assumed that one's understanding is derived from intuitive knowledge. The formulation of a body of principles is said to depend on the use of reason and is thoroughly systematic, while intuitive understanding, although it is sometimes capable of achieving much, is attained by an act of divination, as it were; and since it depends primarily on the *individual's* powers of perception, cognition and so on, it is deemed unreliable. In addition, the former is often considered to be the prototype of masculine knowledge and the latter that of feminine knowledge. (See Hegel's remarks quoted on p. 8 above for a concise expression of the sort of position to which I have been alluding.)

Feminists observe that women have tended to gravitate towards the arts rather than the sciences. Shulamith Firestone, a feminist, finds this natural and explains it, as does the rationalist account of knowledge outlined above, in the following way:

the aesthetic response corresponds with 'female' behaviour. The same terminology can be applied to either: subjective, intuitive, introverted, wishful, dreamy or fantastic, concerned with the subconscious (the id), emotional, even temperamental (hysterical). Correspondingly, the technological response is the masculine response: objective, logical, extroverted, realistic, concerned with the conscious mind (the ego), rational, mechanical, pragmatic and down-to-earth, stable. (*The Dialectic of Sex*, p. 165)

Firestone thinks that this 'cultural division of labour' is unhealthy and criticizes the aesthetic mode for being divorced from reality and the technological mode for the 'falseness and dryness of "objectivity"' (ibid., p. 179). She argues that this division must be abolished and replaced by an 'androgynous' culture, in which the cultural categories, aesthetic and technological (and with them masculinity and femininity), will no longer exist. Nevertheless, she does seem to think (see note 1, p. 32f — as did Hegel, for example — that culture is in any case progressing naturally from the inferior aesthetic mode to the more effective technological mode, in which 'the contingencies of reality are overcome, not through the creation of an alternate reality, but through the mastery of reality's own workings: the laws of nature are exposed, then turned against it, to shape it in accordance with man's conception.' (ibid., p. 165)

Such an account, then, would seem to vindicate the rationalist, 'sexist' view that activities traditionally associated with women and with 'femininity' are inferior. In effect, according to Firestone's characterization of the chief features of the two modes — we shall ignore the difficulties posed by aiming to subsume the multifarious intellectual activities of human beings under these two generalized headings — the implication seems to be that activities in the aesthetic mode are pre-logical, a conception which is, of course, a reverberation of the views we have already met in Hegel and Simmel. The plausibility of this view, however, depends on a spurious contrasting of notions like subjectivity and objectivity on the one hand and logic and intuition on the other.

One difference between scientific and artistic discourse is the way in which we 'test' whether judgements are objective. The character of scientific activity is such that there are straightforward ways in which a theory or an hypothesis may be shown to be true or false. A scientist can specify in advance under what experimental conditions he will either give up or adopt a particular hypothesis as law. The validity of his judgements will be decided by the outcome of his experiments, which will point in either one direction or another. They will decide whether his hypothesis is true or false. In a sense, experiments rather than men decide whether or not an hypothesis is valid. In the case of the arts, however — imagine a work of literary criticism — the desire on the part of a scholar to determine whether a particular view of a novel is 'right' or 'wrong' would strike us as odd. In this situation we are interested not in finding out whether what a man says is right or wrong but in his understanding of, or insight into, the way in which human problems and experiences are treated in the book he is discussing. We are interested in how coherent his thesis is and in whether it gives a cogent account of the novel in question. We may agree with some of the points he makes and may reject others. We may decide that he has not grasped the main point of the novel, but we cannot 'prove' this to him in the way that a scientist may prove to another scientist that his hypotheses are false. There is nothing in this kind of discourse which is analogous to the role an experiment plays in scientific research. Instead we present arguments in favour of one interpretation rather than another: attention is drawn to the force of certain passages, to certain points which have been ignored or over-emphasized and so on.

In an important sense, an experiment can be said to stand on its own. Its results will point to the same conclusions for anyone who is schooled in a particular scientific discipline. It does not matter who executes a particular experiment, and it is enough that it has been executed only once for its results to be considered decisive and final. The case is different in the reading of a novel. When we are interested in what a writer has to say, we are automatically interested in the way others have read the novel. Different individuals bring different concerns and experiences to their reading of a novel and thereby contribute to our understanding of it. Someone may draw attention to a group of ideas in a certain way which would never have occurred to us. When we seek out different interpretations or treatments of a novel, we are concerned not with whether the 'results' of various critics tally but with the light their different views may throw on our understanding of the book. It matters to us, therefore, who says what. An experiment carried out correctly at the last minute by a research assistant is the same experiment as the one that would have been carried out by the professor. But a concert in which one celebrated soprano is replaced by another equally acclaimed one is, in a crucial sense, no longer the same concert even if the programme remains unchanged.

The point is that the role of the subject differs significantly in scientific activity and in artistic activity. Someone who gets the wrong results in chemistry can be taught how to remedy this: he can be taught the techniques and the rules involved in undertaking a successful experiment. On the other hand, while someone who cannot see the point of a poem may be shown the direction in which he should be looking, there are no rules which will enable him to arrive at a better understanding of poetry in the way that rules in chemistry would enable him to be a good chemist. He may simply lack an intuitive awareness of the sense or significance of poetry.

However, none of this means that poetry appreciation, for instance, is devoid of objectivity and logic. A bad appreciation of a poem is one that is contradictory and incoherent, one in which the arguments and ideas proffered relate very superficially to those of the poem discussed. That the perception a subject brings to his reading of a poem is important and plays a crucial role in what we are prepared to call good poetry appreciation does not mean that poetry gives full licence to any individual whim or fancy — to subjectivism.

Firestone, on the other hand, thinks that since the aspect of subjectivity is emphasized in aesthetic discourse, logic and objectivity have been sacrificed. But a painter cannot paint just *anything* without running the risk of being unintelligible both to himself and to his audience. It is important to recognize that art forms may be bounded by rules and conventions without in any way sacrificing the subjectivity and creative instincts of artists. That a piece of music is harmonious and not just a random collection of sounds is something that has to be understood from within the context of a musical community.[4] The existence of a vital community of artists, of an artistic tradition, is what enables us to distinguish sense from nonsense, good art from bad. But then it is important too to see that logic and objectivity in science are not guaranteed by the fact that

[4] For some further discussion of the different ways in which the notion of 'objectivity' enters into the various activities in which human beings are engaged, see Rush Rhees, 'Religion and Language', *Without Answers*, pp. 120–32.

experiments rather than men are the final arbiters of validity. Even in science, an experiment can only say what it does because of the role it already plays in the lives of a community of scientists.[5]

Feminists like Firestone are inclined to suggest that our failure to deal satisfactorily with our social problems stems from the fact that ours is not an androgynous culture. She criticizes artists for being divorced from reality and scientists for ignoring their emotions. But what is wrong with the scientist pontificating on social problems or human psychology is not that he is too dry or too 'objective' in his approach, but that the method he is applying to the study of *human* life is quite inappropriate and should be reserved for the study of natural phenomena. What is needed for imaginative, sensitive work on the problems of human life is not an 'emotional scientist' or, in Firestone's terms, an androgynous being — in this context, a man who gives full expression to his 'feminine' side — but a totally different method of inquiry: that is, a method of inquiry that is not superimposed on the method appropriate for the study of natural phenomena.[6]

Indeed, it is difficult to see why a scientist should be a better *scientist* for being more emotional. He can be a better scientist only by taking more care with his experimental conditions, by using more imagination in the inquiries he is undertaking *and* by recognizing that he is not being scientific — that he cannot be scientific — when he applies the methods of the natural sciences to the problems of social life. His status in the scientific community does not entitle

[5] See Thomas Kuhn's *The Structure of Scientific Revolutions* for some trenchant criticisms of the view that objectivity in science is somehow guaranteed by the existence of straightforwardly testable facts which are thought to stand independently of, and outside, the theoretical frameworks of the scientific community. For what counts as reason or rationality within the context of scientific discourse is not something that lies outside science but is in fact determined by science itself; therefore, no simple psychological demarcation can be made between observational and theoretical propositions, between 'objectivity' and 'subjectivity'.

[6] For a full treatment of this point, see Peter Winch's *The Idea of a Social Science*. Also relevant is Rush Rhees's paper 'Social Engineering', in which he criticizes Karl Popper's view that the methods of the social sciences should be the same as those of the natural sciences (*Without Answers*, pp. 50—68).

him to assume automatically that he has anything interesting or important to say to those whose interests are directed towards the study of human experience. Instead what is required is a certain humility on the part of scientists, acknowledgement that the sphere of scientific activity is strictly limited and cannot be applied indiscriminately to every puzzle with which human beings may be concerned.

Conversely, it is difficult to see why a bad poet would be any the better if he tried to be more 'scientific' in his approach to his work. Writing a poem is not at all like trying to solve a mathematical problem, and there is no reason, therefore, why the respective methods of either should be interchangeable or even helpful to each other. The salient point here is that artists and scientists are not interested in the same kinds of question.

This is the point that Goethe, for example, missed when he criticized Newton's theory of optics, and it is what Firestone misses when she asserts that artistic creativity is, at bottom, the same, though abortive, attempt to change the world as that of scientists. The feminist suggestion that the problems raised by any inquiry in which anyone is likely to be interested, whether it be the formation of black holes or the problems of schizophrenics, will be remedied by the emergence of an 'androgynous' culture — by the fusion of science and art — will not solve anything: it will generate a culture in which there is neither good science nor good art, only confusion. And, furthermore, the very notion of an 'androgynous' culture — the fusion of the 'masculine' and the 'feminine' — is dependent upon the idea of a division of knowledge between the sexes which does not, in any case, exist.

Firestone is prepared to concede, with sexists, that women are intuitive and therefore neither very rational nor logical. Other feminists, however, question the validity of associating women with intuitive knowledge. But precisely because such feminists accept uncritically the rationalist division between intuitive and rational knowledge, they lay great stress on the need for women to be given the opportunity to *reason*. This is why Julia Annas, for example, in

'Mill and the Subjection of Women', criticizes Mill for perpetuating 'the oldest cliché' in the book: that women are intuitive, while men reason.

> If any cliché has done the most harm to the acceptance by men of women as intellectual equals, it is this, and it is distressing to see Mill come out with it. . . . [For this means] it would be appropriate to train boys to go in, at least predominantly, for subjects requiring analytical reasoning, and development of theory, and to train women rather for subjects requiring no sustained reasoning but rather 'human contact' and easily appreciable practical applications. We do not need to be reminded that our educational system is still run largely on these assumptions, and that girls are still notoriously inhibited from going in for subjects on the science and mathematics side, particularly in mixed schools, for fear of being thought too 'masculine'. . . . As long as one admits that women are intuitive and men suited to reasoning, one's best efforts at valuing women's contribution will be patronizing and damaging, encouraging women to think that the most highly regarded intellectual achievements are not for them. (pp. 184—5)

According to Annas's account, the idea that women are intuitive has to be destroyed by giving women full rein in activities that are more 'suited to reasoning'. Like Firestone — and sexists — she accepts that 'rational' activities like science and mathematics, the most highly regarded intellectual activities in our society, are undoubtedly the most intellectually taxing and, further, that they constitute paradigmatic cases of what counts as achievement in other spheres.

But the difficulty with this view of the distinction between rational, 'masculine' and intuitive, 'feminine' knowledge is not the argument that women are inhibited from using their reason but the presumption that 'masculine' activities like science and mathematics are the sole proprietors of reason. The assertion that only men reason — and this is connected with our criticism of Simmel's notion that two theories of knowledge can be applied to the human species — is tantamount to the assertion that it is impossible for men and women to communicate, since women are supposedly arrested at the level of instinctive, animal existence. In any event, whatever the difference between mathematics (say) and feminine accomplishments may be, it does not lie in the fact that the latter do not require reason, for reasoned, intellectual activity does not necessarily involve working according to a water-tight system.

To develop some of the points made above in connection with Firestone, the following should be borne in mind. Contrary to the assumption of many philosophers, the view that a particular accomplishment or skill depends on intuition does not suggest that such knowledge excludes thought and sustained effort. To define a judgement as one based on intuition draws attention to the way in which the facts of a particular situation strike the agent and states that this way of seeing things originates, in a sense, solely with *him*. Consequently, his ideas and judgements are not reducible to a straightforward description of the situation about which he is thinking. And the notion of intuitive knowledge emphasizes that such knowledge cannot be learned from books or through formal study but only through *experience*. Every new initiate must learn for himself, in his distinctly individual way, what is right and what is wrong. (This is why such training is sometimes referred to as 'vocational' training.) The distinction, then, between scientific or 'rational' knowledge and intuitive knowledge is a question not so much of different reasoning processes or theories of knowledge as of the peculiarly different roles which the notions of learning and teaching assume in the two contexts.

Wittgenstein, in discussing a rather different problem in *Philosophical Investigations*, makes this point as follows:

Is there such a thing as 'expert judgement' about the genuineness of expressions of feeling? — Even here, there are those whose judgement is 'better' and those whose judgement is 'worse'.

Correcter prognoses will generally issue from the judgements of those with better knowledge of mankind.

Can one learn this knowledge? Yes; some can. Not, however, by taking a course in it, but through 'experience'. — Can someone else be a man's teacher in this? Certainly. From time to time he gives him the right *tip*. This is what 'learning' and 'teaching' are like here. — What one acquires is not a technique; one learns correct judgements. There are also rules, but they do not form a system, and only experienced people can apply them right. Unlike calculating rules.

What is most difficult here is to put this indefiniteness, correctly and unfalsified, into words. (IIxi, p. 227)

This passage from Wittgenstein is illuminating for reasons which go far beyond the particular issue he is considering, for it says something of crucial significance about the way in which accomplishments in the non-scientific sphere are acquired. The emphasis on experience is important because the kind of perception appropriate to, and the rules that govern, literary criticism (say) cannot provide a formulaic guide to how to be philosophically critical or politically astute, how to be a fine cellist and so on. Moreover, it would be an expression of prejudice to say that none of these activities involves sustained reasoning but only 'easily appreciable practical applications' (Annas) or the flights of fancy implied by Firestone simply because an adequate characterization of them cannot turn on the fact that they depend strictly on analytical reasoning and the development of theory. Nor should we be tempted to think that the more the methods of non-scientific activities resemble scientific methods, the greater the progress they are making.

To see this is to see that the deprecatory attitude towards the so-called intuitive faculty of women is symptomatic of a more general prejudice against those forms of knowledge that are non-scientific in character. It is more to the point, therefore, to show not that women too can excel in scientific activities but that science is not an absolute gauge of what counts as knowledge. It is necessary to see that insistence on the argument that women must be given access to scientific study in order to display their intellectual prowess only nourishes the soil in which prejudice against women first finds root; it does not destroy it. This point will become clearer by considering, quite apart from issues directly concerning women, how a pre-occupation with laws and theories — with scientific method — may reveal lack of intelligence and deep thought.

In philosophy, for instance, a preoccupation with the methods of science has resulted, as is impressively shown by Wittgenstein's later philosophy, not in clarification of but in a total misunderstanding of the sort of investigation required to deal with philosophical difficulties. His later notion of *meaning as use* constitutes a radical departure from the ideas of the *Tractatus* period because it involves combating the temptation to think of language as an exact calculus. The view that there must be some essential ingredient which justifies our using the same word in a variety of ways, Wittgenstein argues, is a shadow cast upon our language by science. The whole search in philosophy for universals, substances, essences is a symptom of this preoccupation with the methods of science, of 'the craving for generality and the contemptuous attitude towards the particular case'.[7] Hence the idea of the exactitude of logic, so central to the *Tractatus*, creeps into philosophy because we fail to see that logic does not treat language in the way in which a natural science treats natural phenomena.[8]

---

[7] Our craving for generality has another main source: our preoccupation with the method of science. I mean the method of reducing the explanation of natural phenomena to the smallest possible number of primitive natural laws; and, in mathematics, of unifying the treatment of different topics by using a generalization. Philosophers constantly see the method of science before their eyes, and are irresistibly tempted to ask and answer questions in the way science does. This tendency . . . leads the philosopher into complete darkness. . . .

Instead of 'craving for generality' I could also have said 'the contemptuous attitude towards the particular case'. If, e.g., someone tries to explain the concept of number and tells us that such and such a definition will not do or is clumsy because it only applies to, say, finite cardinals I should answer that the mere fact that he could have given such a limited definition makes this definition extremely important to us. (Elegance is *not* what we are trying for.) For why should what finite and transfinite numbers have in common be more interesting to us than what distinguishes them? Or rather, I should not have said 'why should it be more interesting to us?' — it *isn't*; and this characterizes our way of thinking. (Wittgenstein, *The Blue and Brown Books*, pp. 18—19)

[8] Cf. what he says about his view of philosophy in the *Tractatus* period:

F. P. Ramsey once emphasized in conversation with me that logic was 'a normative science'. I do not know exactly what he had in mind but it was

Wittgenstein argues that we require a grammatical investigation, an investigation into the way we *use* our concepts and of the language games in which they appear. Only by looking at the use of words can we discover the complex relations between the quite ordinary ways in which we speak and act in common discourse. The philosophical difficulties have to be met and worked through each time. There is no 'simplification' or 'theory development' which will make the problems any less difficult and therefore no laws or theorems which will enable us to carry out the whole exercise more simply, without having to go through all the troubles which have constantly beset philosophers. One has missed the kind of difficulty that is raised in philosophy if one imagines that philosophical study is directed towards 'theory development'.

Of course, philosophy is only one instance among many of an intellectual activity which requires sustained reasoning and enormous concentration but in which the aping of scientific method does not necessarily display greater intelligence and is, in fact, positively detrimental. According to Wittgenstein's conception of philosophy, there is no reason why the traditional education provided for girls to which Annas alludes — I take it she is thinking of an emphasis on

---

doubtless closely related to what only dawned on me later: namely, that in philosophy we often *compare* the use of words with games and calculi which have fixed rules, but cannot say that someone who is using language *must* be playing such a game. — But if you say that our languages only *approximate* to such calculi you are standing on the very brink of a misunderstanding. For then it may look as if what we were talking about were an *ideal* language. As if our logic were, so to speak, a logic for a vacuum. — Whereas logic does not treat of language — or of thought — in the sense in which a natural science treats of a natural phenomenon, and the most that can be said is that we *construct* ideal languages. But here the word 'ideal' is liable to mislead, for it sounds as if these languages were better, more perfect, than our everyday language; and as if it took the logician to shew people at last what a proper sentence looked like.

All this, however, can only appear in the right light when one has attained greater clarity about the concepts of understanding, meaning and thinking. For it will then also become clear what can lead us (and did lead me) to think that if anyone utters a sentence and *means* or *understands* it he is operating a calculus according to definite rules. (*Philosophical Investigations*, para. 81)

the arts and the humanities — should not offer opportunities for the display of great intellect. In opposition to Annas, I suggest that the real difficulty confronting men who find it hard to accept women as intellectual equals is not the intelligence level of women but the inveterate conviction of our culture that a man has not thought hard about an issue unless his thought has culminated in a sophisticated system of laws and theories.

Indeed, it is this very notion that has played an important part in the emergence of a prejudice that has made it difficult for anthropologists to assign 'substantial feats of intellect' to primitive peoples. This is shown with some force in Thomas Gladwin's interestingly drawn contrast between Trukese methods of navigation and European ones (although Gladwin does not identify the reasons for the prejudice in the way I do). Trukese techniques of navigation do not include even a compass, to say nothing of chronometers, sextants or star tables, but the Trukese are able to make voyages spanning over a hundred miles of open ocean. At first sight, it does look as if these men have a sort of sixth sense, but as Gladwin explains in 'Cultural and Logical Process':

Essentially the navigator relies on dead reckoning. He sets his course by the rising and setting of stars, having memorized for this purpose the knowledge gleaned from generations of observations of the direction in which stars rise and fall through the seasons. A heading toward a given island, when leaving another island, is set a particular season a trifle to the left, or perhaps the right, of a certain star at its setting or rising. Through the night a succession of such stars will rise or fall, and each will be noted and the course checked. Between stars, or when the stars are not visible due to daylight or storm, the course is held constant by noting the direction of the wind and the waves. A good navigator can tell by observing wave patterns when the wind is shifting its direction and speed, and by how much. In a dark and starless night the navigator can even tell these things from the sound of waves as they lap upon the side of the canoe's hull, and the feel of the boat as it travels through the water. All of these complex perceptions — visual, auditory, kinaesthetic — are combined with vast amounts of data stored in memory, and the whole is integrated into a slight increase or decrease in pressure on the

steering paddle, or a grunted instruction to slack off the sail a trifle. . . .
The significance of each observation is established by a comparison
with remembered observations from past experience, a result of training.
This training and experience also determines unequivocally what
phenomena shall be observed and what is ignored. The selection and
accumulation of necessary information thus requires a minimum of
reasoning or logical choice. (pp. 112—14)

And, moreover, while

the Trukese navigator can point to his destination over the horizon . . .
he cannot possibly put into words all of the myriad perceptions which
have led him to be sure at that moment where the island lies. This is not
merely because the Trukese are unaccustomed to describing in words
what they are doing. The simultaneous integration of several discrete
thought processes defies verbalization. The navigator can probably
inventory all of the factors to which he must be alert, but the process
whereby these are weighted and combined is both complex and fluid.
(p. 117)[9]

By contrast, the European navigator

will . . . be governed by navigational and other techniques which are
concrete applications of basic principles. Some of these . . . are highly
abstract in nature . . . the navigator may or may not understand all of
the theory which lies behind his techniques, but they had originally to
be developed through an explicit sequence of logical steps. However,
once the European navigator has developed his operating plan and has
available the appropriate technical resources, the implementation and
monitoring of his navigation can be accomplished with a minimum of
thought. (p. 117)

This account of Trukese navigational methods has a twofold
significance. First, it shows that 'theory development' cannot be
taken as an absolute criterion of intellectual prowess. Second, coming
to terms with this point is not a matter of merely being kinder and

---

[9] See Wittgenstein's remark cited on pp. 41—2.

more tolerant to women and to primitives but necessitates a radical transformation of the epistemological assumptions implicit in both sexism and feminism and in racism.

Besides, the prestige of scientific activities in our society is not related primarily to the supposedly greater intellectual powers of scientists; it is related to the fact that ours is a mass industrial society, in which power is increasingly concentrated in the hands of technocrats and technicians.[10] The prestige of science connects with the possibilities it apparently offers us of maintaining in full momentum a certain kind of economic and social system.

It hardly needs to be added that the enormous emphasis on 'scientific' training, even for boys, is related too to the demands of our highly industrialized, technological society, to the fact that as a society we no longer have any use for thatchers, wheelwrights, potters and so on but only for people who will passively sit at and maintain machines capable of manufacturing anything from roof tiles to plastic flowers. The fact that abstract theorizing is not always helpful or appropriate is further reflected in the fact that there used to be many trades and crafts, the training for which consisted in serving an apprenticeship. The number of such trades and crafts and the need for this sort of education has decreased considerably and will continue to do so with the ever-increasing pace of technological advance and the increase in mass-produced goods.[11]

Annas thinks it is harmful to think of women as intuitive. However, the prejudice we are up against here is not one against women but is connected with a confused notion of reason. The feminist complaint that women are not given access to 'rational', 'masculine' activities therefore leaves intact the very soil in which

---

[10] See, e.g., Simone Weil's two essays 'Prospects' and 'Reflections concerning Technocracy, National-Socialism, the USSR and Certain Other Matters' in *Oppression and Liberty*.

[11] This, in turn, is connected with the rationalization and bureaucratization of modern life, necessary to meet the demands of running a mass society. For some suggestive remarks, see Max Weber, 'The "Rationalization" of Education and Training', in H. H. Gerth and C. Wright Mills, *From Max Weber*.

the sexist prejudice against women is rooted. Hence feminist argument hardly touches, if at all, the ground in which such prejudice finds life and breath. The point that such prejudice is related to a lack of understanding about the nature of intuitive knowledge can be clarified by considering the following discussion of Sturt's work, which shows clearly that the notion of rationality or reason can be understood only in the context of the particular activity with which one is concerned and, further, that intuitive knowledge, like other forms of knowledge, is acquired only through learning and training.

In his book *The Wheelwright's Shop*, George Sturt gives an interesting account of the indispensable role that experience plays in the learning of a craft. From the point of view of an outsider, the wheelwright's ability to discern, almost at a glance, that 'likely-looking timber' is unfit for a job appears to rest on a sort of marvellous power. Moreover, his inability to articulate his reasons for executing something in one way rather than another is apt to make us think of him as stupid. However, through Sturt's careful and detailed description of the training that the wheelwright undergoes, we gradually become initiated into a way of looking at the craft that demonstrates that nothing the wheelwright does is merely arbitrary; everything is related to a complex and intricate body of knowledge. Sensitive to the likely prejudices of his reader, Sturt forces us to appreciate that the wheelwright's achievements, although they cannot be accounted for in terms of any theory or law, are nevertheless achievements of an order that demands the highest respect.

There was nothing for it but practice and experience of every difficulty. Reasoned science for us did not exist. 'Theirs not to reason why.' What we had to do was to live up to the local wisdom of our kind; to follow the customs, and work to the measurements, which had been tested and corrected long before our time in every village shop all across the country. A wheelwright's brain had to fit itself to this by dint of growing into it . . . Science? Our two-foot rules took us no nearer to exactness than the sixteenth of an inch: we used to make or adjust special gauges for the nicer work; but very soon a stage was reached when eye and hand were left to their own cleverness, with no guide to help them. So the work was more of an art — a very fascinating art — than a science; and in this art, as I say, the brain had its share. A good wheelwright knew by art but not by reasoning the proportion to keep between spokes and felloes . . . He felt it, in his bones. It was a perception with him. But there was no science in it; no reasoning. Every detail stood by itself, and had to be learnt by trial and error or by tradition. (pp. 19—20)

It is tempting to think that the use of precision instruments might nevertheless have facilitated the work of the wheelwright, but this would be wrong, I think. It would be wrong for the same reason that the use of a chemical balance in her kitchen would not make an inferior cook a better one because in the kitchen the role that the accuracy of measurements plays is not comparable with its importance in a chemistry experiment. For example, while it is obviously important to mix the ingredients in the right proportions if a good cake is to be made, it is possible to juggle with them in order to obtain a certain effect in a way that would be quite unacceptable in an experiment. Moreover, the reasons why someone may be a bad cook, in contradistinction to being a bad chemist, may have nothing to do with inaccurate measurements. In some cases it may actually result from following a recipe rigidly and not knowing how to adapt it to suit one's own particular tastes and circumstances. Such knowledge, however, depends on practice and on the help of those who are experienced cooks.

When Sturt writes, 'A good wheelwright knew by art but not by reasoning . . .', he is clearly not saying that the wheelwright knew by virtue of a sort of magical power — 'in this art, as I say, the brain had its share' — but he is emphasizing that what the wheelwright knew was something that depended, necessarily, on experience:[12]

---

[12] It is interesting to contrast Sturt's description of the wheelwright's knowledge with Thomas Hardy's account of Winterbourne's success with planting trees in *The Woodlanders*. Hardy makes it look as if intuitive knowledge were somehow magical:

He had a marvellous power of making trees grow. Although he would seem to shovel in the earth quite carelessly there was a sort of sympathy between

I have known old-fashioned workmen refuse to use likely-looking timber because they held it to be unfit for the job.

And they knew. The skilled workman was the final judge. Under the plane (it is little used now) or under the axe (it is all but obsolete) timber disclosed qualities hardly to be found otherwise. My own eyes know because my own hands have felt, but I cannot teach an outsider the difference between ash that is 'tough as whipcord' and ash that is 'frow as a carrot', or 'doaty', or 'biscuity'. In oak, in beech, these differences are equally plain, *yet only to those who have been initiated by practical work.* (p. 24; my italics)

Despite such keenness of perception on the part of the wheelwright, Sturt readily admits that the wheelwright's knowledge cannot be called scientific.

The nature of this knowledge should be noted. It was set out in no book. It was not scientific. I never met a man who professed any other than an empirical acquaintance with the waggon-builder's lore . . . The lore was a tangled network of country prejudices, whose reasons were known in some respects here, in others there, and so on. In farm-yard, in tap-room, at market, the details were discussed over and over again; they were gathered together for remembrance in village workshop; carters, smiths, farmers, wheel-makers, in thousands handed on each his own little bit of understanding, passing it to his son or to the wheelwright of the day, linking up the centuries. But for the most part the details were but dimly understood; the whole body of knowledge was a mystery, a piece of folk knowledge, residing in the folk collectively, but never wholly in any individual. (p. 79)

That the 'lore' was a 'tangled network' should not surprise us, for we learn further that the wheelwright 'knew each customer and his needs; understood his carters and his horses and the nature of his

---

himself and the fir, oak, or beech that he was operating on; so that the roots took hold of the soil in a few days. When, on the other hand, any of the journeymen planted, although they seemed to go through an identically similar process, one quarter of the trees would die away during the ensuing August. (*The Woodlanders*, p. 68)

land; and finally took a pride in providing exactly what was wanted in every case' (p. 54). This emphasis on the *particular and individual* case explains most satisfactorily why the wheelwright's knowledge can never be scientific knowledge and why 'theory development' is of no interest to him — not because he does not reason or because he is intellectually stunted but because it is not *this* that is required for making good wheels and waggons. Nothing abstract and merely analytical will help him to learn what is or is not important as regards the requirements of a particular customer. He has to get back to rough ground, so to speak, to be sure that his waggon is of the highest quality. His senses, particularly those of sight and touch, have to be cultivated and nurtured not merely to save him from crashing into other people or from burning himself, but to distinguish the subtle differences between varying timbers. He has to be wholly alert and attentive, to make a sustained effort to be mindful of his work, so that when he has completed the four wheels he will not be faced with a lopsided waggon. All this is fairly obvious, but it is extraordinary how easily we forget how much learning is required even for what may seem to be the simplest tasks. In this connection, Tolstoy's vivid description of Levin learning to scythe — note particularly the contrast between Levin's awkward and clumsy movements and the graceful ones of the old man — is a striking reminder of this last point (see *Anna Karenina*, pp. 268—76).

Clearly, it would be impossible for the wheelwright, working as he does in wood, to know all that he needed to know about the different timbers if he did not live a life that was close to nature. Sturt recalls grimly how he foolishly bought some oaks from a certain hollow which had 'a nasty trick of going "foxy-hearted" ' despite their beautiful appearance. He remarks that his father and grandfather would not have made this mistake, for they would have known that the rich soil in which the trees grew would have adversely affected them. 'They knew "England" in a more intimate way.' (p. 26) And Sturt's recognition that he has lost some of the folk knowledge about the importance of the soil in which timber grows rightly contradicts Hegel's insistence that the desire to live close to nature fails to acknowledge that all knowledge requires the subject—object dyad.

Certainly, what we discover from Sturt about the wheelwright is that someone who thought he might learn about timbers without living in a kind of intimacy with nature would be making a stupid mistake.

Sturt's study of the wheelwright's shop, then, is interesting, among other reasons, because it is a reminder that reason, or rationality, shows itself in people's lives in many different ways. The supposition that analytical reasoning and the development of theory are indispensable features of true knowledge does not demonstrate that women have been inhibited from using their reason: rather, it is a prejudice built on the notion that any activity, whether it is scientific or not, must aim at general laws and rational principles. Scientific method gives us the answer to what we must look for if we wish to master life technically. It gives us the means only to an understanding of the natural world, and, whatever the value of such understanding, it is strictly limited in application. In certain cases, to shrink away from theorizing and systematizing may therefore offer a profound insight into the nature of the problems one is considering. Wittgenstein's philosophic method, as we saw above, is an obvious case in point. Hence to assume *a priori*, as both feminists and their opponents are prone to do, that it is disadvantageous not to be well disposed to analytical reasoning and the development of theory is to ignore the enormous diversity of the pursuits or tasks in which human beings are commonly engaged. And, crucially, it is evident that the activities of the public sphere cannot all be categorized according to the schema suggested by Kant and Hegel.

Feminism is predicated on the demand that women must no longer be confined to the home if they are to lead active, fulfilling lives. This demand throws up enormous difficulties but, suffice it to say for the moment, the idea that women rightly belong in the private sphere is wholly compatible with the notion that women, like men, are not animals. The activities of the private sphere, no less than those of the public realm, can be executed only by human beings.

Moreover, if one remembers that until very recently the bearing and rearing of children was insisted upon as the peculiar destiny of women, it is no mere accident or silly prejudice that women have been inhibited from learning to respond to, and deal with, situations at the level of the rational and the universal. Indeed, it is crucial that, for the most part, women are taught to think at the level of the particular and the affective because the relationship between mother and child is a relationship between two individual human beings. The mother loves her child (or is expected to) simply because it is her child, and equally the child loves its mother (or is expected to) simply because she is its mother. And however primitive or instinctive the relationship between mother and child may seem to us, it never occurs automatically. If the conceptual background and the affective surroundings that make it both possible and intelligible for a woman to take up an attitude of love towards her infant are not present, there will be no such love. John Bowlby's classic study on maternal deprivation, *Maternal Care and Mental Health*, is a tragic reminder of this. Deep maternal love is a possibility for many women in our society only because of the way we think and act in all sorts of other situations. Disastrously, however, these ways of thinking and acting are being continually eroded by the wholesale emphasis in our society on methods and procedures appropriate to spheres of activities dominated by scientific method, technology and productivity goals.

Sheila Kitzinger, for instance, draws attention to the inevitable difficulties that this emphasis causes for women. In a discussion of the special demands the role of mothering makes of women in *Women as Mothers*, she cites Helene Lopata, who points out that school and work teach young women to be 'task-oriented, to measure accomplishments in terms of a finished product, and to organize it in blocks of time within a specialized division of labour'; but this only serves to confound them as they face the problems they have to try to 'solve' as mothers because the 'care of infants and the socialization of children are . . . highly emotional processes . . . and there is no perfect procedure for them' (p. 34). Moreover, adds Kitzinger, 'as the child grows it requires different things from its mother and this means that she can never perfect her techniques, but must remain flexible and capable of adapting to a changed situation.' It would seem, then, that it is *not* so 'outrageously paradoxical to deny woman all activity in public affairs, to shut her out of masculine careers . . . and then to entrust to her the most delicate and the most serious undertaking of all: the moulding of a human being' (Beauvoir, *The Second Sex*, p. 501). On the contrary, the demand of feminists like Beauvoir that women ought to be permitted to become more fully and more directly involved in 'masculine' activities has unfortunately exacerbated their difficulties as mothers, because they are taught to focus their attention exclusively on methods which are alien to, and counter-productive in, the concerns and responsibilities they face in their relations with their children.

It is vital for motherhood (as it is commonly understood) that there are people who are aware that there are many things in life which can neither be learned from books nor understood from the position of an outsider. It is only because we realize that acting with rigid consistency is not always a sign of reasonable and appropriate behaviour that we do not think a mother is stupid when, for example, we see her, from one day to the next, making delicate adjustments in the care of her infant which other people would not think worth while. Hence the fact that mothers are seldom interested in Kantian ethics (Weininger) probably says less for Kant than it does for the mothers. Equally, we are not surprised when we find that many mothers are extremely hesitant about concocting theories about how other people should bring up their children and are sceptical about the advice thrust upon them by the 'experts'. For however spontaneous, natural or intuitive the response of a woman to her infant may seem to be, it should not be forgotten that in that one response there lives a wealth of experience and learning about individual children that often extends beyond the individual to her foremothers. When such experience and learning do not form the basis of a woman's maternal responses, a situation like the present one arises, in which women and their unfortunate offspring become victims of speculative theories of child care which change from one generation to the next. That is why Rudolph Schaffer, for example — and, indeed, the whole band of those who advocate standardizing and 'making scientific' our methods of child-rearing — is wrong to suggest, in his book *Mothering*:

There is, in fact, no reason why bringing up the under-fives should not also be guided by firm knowledge scientifically established rather than depend, as happens at present, on fashion, prejudice and what grandmother says. The parent—child relationship need be no more immune from properly conducted objective inquiry than the movements of the planets or the structure of DNA — even if its analysis presents problems of far greater complexity. (p. 11)[13]

I do not wish to be taken as saying that practices of child care based on tradition are always immune from criticism, but rather that a practice can be based on tradition and, for that very reason, may count as knowledge. This is the point that Schaffer misses. Schaffer aims to provide women with scientific certainty that their method of child-rearing will be successful. Apart from the fact that it is foolish to seek 'certainty' in one's relations with others, this is pseudo-science because the relation between individuals is, by definition, something that cannot become subsumed under a statistical generalization. Once that is done, the aspect of individuality vanishes.

What I have been emphasizing, then, is that woman's intuitive ability is not an innate faculty but rather one that comes only with a certain sort of training. True, many feminists have recognized this. What they have failed to see, however, is that it is because we are talking here of something that can be learned, and for which there are rules for proceeding, that we have a case which can appropriately be described as rational behaviour. Thus to say that although women intuit, they are also capable of reasoning is to resort to pleonasm. What feminists need to acknowledge is that the whole rationalist enterprise was able to get off the ground only because a spurious

[13] And for some criticism of the idea that the difference between human beings and DNA (say) is merely a difference in complexity, see Peter Winch, *The Idea of a Social Science*, chapter 3.

contrast was made between rationality and intuition, between reason and emotion. How far they are from seeing this, however, emerges quite clearly from Shulamith Firestone's account of the 'dialectics of cultural history', for example, which depends for its plausibility on, among other things, an antagonistic relationship between two supposedly independent forces: reason and emotion.

In sum, we have seen so far that the idea that reasoning is the peculiar prerogative of masculine pursuits, and therefore of the male sex, is not so much a prejudice against women as a conviction built on the notion that reason is a distinct faculty present only in those pursuits for which there are no parallels in the animal world. For what makes something distinctly human is not its absence from animal life but its place in a form of human life of which it constitutes a part. Therefore the humanity, or rational nature, of women is to be found precisely in the existence of procreation and child-rearing in *surroundings or contexts of thoughts and actions* which are decidedly peculiar to human beings. Thus the idea of sexists that women cannot reason and the idea of feminists that they do not reason because they have never been given the necessary educational opportunities rest on the same misconceptions.

Tagged - intuitive

4

Sex Differences, Socialization and Internal Relations

Generally, discussions about problems raised by sex differences scarcely seem to centre on the sorts of issues I have been discussing. Instead the traditional feminist approach has been to examine arguments of a quite different kind — those of a sociological or political nature. Feminists' criticism of sexist biological and psychological theories about the nature of women rests, for the most part, on the view that such theories tend to reflect and rationalize the existing socially and economically inferior status of women. Now, it might be argued that although they do not tackle the philosophical issues, they do at least cast doubt on sexist arguments by showing that since the position of women could be and has been different, there must be something amiss with the sexist's reasoning. There can be little doubt that feminists do succeed in showing that there is something unjust in sexism, but in doing this they encourage a view of sexism which makes it impossible to see the motivation for adopting a sexist position as anything other than a sort of will to power. And in failing to come to terms with other important considerations, they urge women along a false trail to liberation. This error rests on the problematic way in which they interpret the nature of femininity as a social construct.

Feminists have been unanimous in their view that differentiation between men and women can be justified only if a male nature and a female nature can be separately identified. Perhaps because they have taken Freud as their arch-enemy, they have readily assumed that this question is essentially an empirical one; from him they have borrowed a methodological bias according to which it is argued that any true foundation for distinguishing masculinity and femininity must be based on the biological sciences. In Freudian terms, for instance, this amounts to the assertion that men are active and aggressive because the male sexual organ is active during coition; conversely, women are passive and apparently masochistic because the female libido is located in the vagina.[1] Thus it is assumed that the argument 'Anatomy is destiny' is valid only if the relation between a person's biological sex and his gender characteristics is a *causal* one.

Consequently, feminists argue there are two possible methods of inquiry into the nature of femininity. Either we wait until biological research is able to tell us something decisive about the physiological determinants of gender characteristics — the possibility, perhaps, of a one-to-one relation between each gender characteristic and a chemical bodily change — or we undertake an historical or anthropological study into the nature of femininity, confident that if femininity is not a chimera, then at least certain of its features will be universally revealed. The category of universality assumes significance here because the notion of a non-arbitrary relation between two factors, no matter what they might be, is *ipso facto* thought to be one that is law-like.

The question, then, remains how one is to understand deviations in behavioural patterns. For feminists the knowledge that there are divergences in the way the notion of femininity has been understood from culture to culture and in different historical periods is enough to suggest that biology is unlikely to prove that gender is physiologically determined, for a universal law cannot reasonably

[1] Sigmund Freud, 'Femininity', lecture 33 of *New Introductory Lectures on Psychoanalysis*, vol. 22 of *The Standard Edition of the Complete Psychological Works*. Freud equates masculine with active and feminine with passive. According to him, the little girl discovers in early childhood that she lacks something possessed by the boy. Because of this she believes that she has been castrated and deals with this shock by sublimating the wish for a penis in the wish for a child. With the sublimation of the wish for a penis, the woman is supposed also to move from enjoyment of clitoral to vaginal orgasm, since the latter is apparently more passive and therefore more feminine in nature.

admit any exceptions. And, crucially, they believe that they have destroyed the Freudian myth that women are passive by proving on factual grounds that the female libido is located not primarily, if at all, in the vagina, but in the clitoris.[2] At any rate, their general conclusion is that since there is no causal relation between sex and gender, and since all differences between men and women seem to be thoroughly social, the differences between men and women are not fundamental differences of nature. Concluding her discussion of the significance of the biological research on sex differences, Kate Millett, for example, writes in *Sexual Politics*:

Since patriarchy's biological foundations appear to be so very insecure, one has some cause to admire the strength of a 'socialization' which can continue a universal condition 'on faith alone', as it were, or through an acquired value system exclusively. What does seem decisive in assuring the maintenance of the temperamental differences between the sexes is the conditioning of early childhood. (p. 31)

Therefore,

Whatever the 'real' differences between the sexes may be, we are not likely to know them until the sexes are treated differently, that is alike. (p. 29)

Now, while feminists are absolutely right to point out that being a woman is a social and cultural matter rather than simply biological one, they have not grasped the real significance of this claim. The fact that our notion of femininity is a culturally biased one does not, by itself, destroy the legitimacy of the notion. This would be the case only if the question of a female nature involved an inquiry into the nature of a physical entity and was something that could be decided by science. So even if the empirical evidence for sex differences is

[2] See, for example, Mary Jane Sherfey, 'On the Nature of Female Sexuality'. Feminists fail to see, however, that the notion of passivity that is at stake here is an epistemological and not a biological one. I shall return to the question of 'feminine' passivity in chapter 5.

inconclusive or even negative, such empirical inquiry is irrelevant to the issue. The realization that the notion of femininity does differ from society to society should instead be an indication that any attempt to account for sex differences scientifically in terms of one law or another itself rests on a confusion. Indeed, it is precisely because the very nature of social life consists in different and competing ways of life, each offering a different account of the intelligibility of things, that we would *not* expect our notion of femininity to be universally applicable. That it does not hold universally does not mean it is merely arbitrary,[3] for universality does not count as a criterion of legitimacy in this kind of case.

The sorts of conceptual confusion on both sides of the debate over sex differences are well illustrated by Peter Winch in his book *The Idea of a Social Science*. Winch argues that the method of the natural sciences — the search for universal laws — is inappropriate for the study of human life because the rules that govern it are as diverse as the multifarious activities in which human beings are engaged and cannot be subsumed, therefore, into a neat and tidy system of empirical generalizations. The philosophical basis for Winch's argument derives from Wittgenstein's perception that the meaning of a word is to be found in its use. Since the use of a word presupposes a social context, it is always there that we have to look for clarification of its meaning. And since the rules governing the use of a word may differ from context to context, it is only when we are quite clear which rules or criteria govern certain assertions that we can be sure that we have understood what is being said. This means that the kind of puzzlement we feel, for example, about whether there is a female nature, or about what someone means by appealing to such a conception, will be resolved satisfactorily only by elucidating the internal relations, if there are any, that obtain between the variety of things we call feminine. Our difficulty here is to be clear about what we mean, to try to understand the nature of our confusion.

---

[3] I shall return to this notion of 'arbitrariness' in chapter 5.

One way of putting this is to say that not all questions of the form 'Does X exist?' are on the same level. For example, the question 'Are there neutrons?' is a radically different kind of question from 'Is there a God?' Some understanding of what this difference is will entail looking at many things: for instance, the situations in which people ask such questions; the sorts of answers they find meaningful or intelligible; what conditions will or could count as verification; the sort of difference it makes to their lives as a whole if the answer is in the negative; whether it would be appropriate to talk of something needing to be discovered in both cases; and so on. Coming face to face with questions of this sort and with the very different kinds of answers ordinarily given in the two cases reminds us that the problem of whether or not God exists cannot be solved empirically and does not raise issues that physics is either interested in or could answer.

Think of the case of a parent whose child has just died. The doctor gives the reason for the death, and the mother simply keeps repeating, 'Why? Why?' Clearly, the doctor does not assume that the reasons he has given are inadequate and that she wishes to know the medical causes of the case in greater detail. The question 'Why?' is put by the woman in order to gain some *sense* of the event, to try to come to terms with it, perhaps in a way that could give it meaning. This difficulty — the meaning of death — is something that biochemistry does not try to solve.

Now, the difference between the sets of questions in the two examples given above is what in philosophical idiom may be described as a difference in *grammar*. That is to say, the difficulties or the issues raised by a simple question or proposition — the question 'Why?', for example — can be radically different when two quite different systems of discourse are taken as their frames of reference. Thus someone who is worried about his masculinity is not generally worried about the number of Y chromosomes he may or may not have. He is thinking about his relation to women and to other men, about marriage, about children, about social problems perhaps, about his life as a whole and the meaning it has for him. He is thinking too of the actual physical nature of birth and sex.[4] That this is what is going on is shown by Margaret Mead in her cross-cultural studies of sex and temperament (see *Male and Female*). Hence it is important to see that no matter what biologists may find out about sex differences, such research cannot answer these questions. What we are being invited to do, when faced with a sexual stereotype, is to think of the situations in which it might be made and about the notions which might be involved.

It is only fair to say that feminists do admit that our notions of femininity are associated with the way in which we think about all sorts of other things. Indeed, they have chosen as their slogan 'The personal is political.' Sexual relations, the organization of work in society, our behaviour towards children and so on are seen to be intertwined in a way that is significant for the maintenance of a patriarchal society. And precisely because being a woman is a social matter, radical feminists empasize that changes in the role and status of women cannot be achieved through piecemeal reforms, but will necessarily entail the transformation of our society as a whole. Even so, there are difficulties with the way in which feminists construe the relation between femininity and society, difficulties which can be summed up by saying that they fail to see this relation as an *internal* one.

As already noted, feminists assume that our notion of femininity can be legitimate only if it is totally independent of any cultural bias and therefore universally applicable. From this they argue that since there is no necessary (in the sense of inevitable) connection between sex and gender, any contingent connection there is must be a result of socialization. By paying attention to the socialization process, they feel able to account for the diversity of the roles and behaviour of men and women in different cultures and at different historical periods. They argue that because all significant differences between men and women are thoroughly social, the psychosexual distinctions made between the two groups serve only to justify their present

[4] This point is developed more fully in chapter 5.

political relationships. Our notions of femininity and the socialization that goes with it are instrumental in maintaining certain power relations between the sexes. Roles are identified as instruments of oppression which prevent women from expressing their individuality. Consequently, at least one aim of feminism is the abolition of socialization.

According to feminist accounts, a woman finds that every move she makes expresses a role imposed upon her by patriarchy for its own benefit. Through socialization, she is coerced to subsume within herself, as it were, the prescriptions of society and to make them the basis of her behaviour, thus creating the illusion of a female nature. Socialization is seen simply as the systematic denial of our supposed absolute individuality and liberty by the constraints imposed by social roles.

The crucial notion here is that of 'constraint'. For the recognition that femininity is a *social* fact is, according to the feminist view, tantamount to the assertion that women have always been oppressed by society. Why this should necessarily be so is evident in Durkheim's conception of socialization, a conception still very prevalent among writers on role theory.[5] As he puts it in *The Rules of Sociological Method*:

A social fact is to be recognized by the power of external coercion which it exercises or is capable of exercising over individuals, and the presence of this power may be recognized in its turn either by the existence of some specific sanction or by the resistance offered against every individual effort that tends to violate it. (p. 10)

From this, he concludes that:

---

[5] See for example, Gerry Cohen, 'Belief and Roles'. Cohen does, in fact, reject the view of sociologists like Goffman and Dahrendorf, who maintain that the self is nothing more than the sum of the roles that it plays. Nevertheless, he is in essential agreement with them over the view that roles are instruments of oppression, differing from these sociologists in believing that one may reasonably look forward to a time when 'real, individual men will be able to confront one another, and themselves, without the mediation of any institutions' (p. 32).

the aim of education is, precisely, the socialization of the human being; the process of education, therefore, gives us in a nutshell the historical fashion in which the social being is constituted. This unremitting pressure to which the child is subjected is the very pressure of the social milieu which tends to fashion him in its own image, and of which parents and teachers are merely the representatives and intermediaries. (p. 6)

Hence the relation between the individual and any authority — priests, teachers, husbands, fathers and so on — is construed always in political terms, in terms of the will of one individual in opposition to that of another. But whereas Durkheim thought such constraint a necessary evil if men are to live together, as did Hobbes, feminists regard it as an evil, pure and simple. Thus they refuse to see feminine roles as anything other than alien categories which coerce the individual and force her to abandon her 'real self'. Since all that is social is held to be artificial by its very nature, the search for sex differences has to direct itself to something that is pre- or post-cultural. This is why it is thought that the question of the existence of a female nature will be decided either when women are freed from 'the tyranny of sexual—social category' (Millett, *Sexual Politics*, p. 363) or by biology.

In an obvious sense, the individual who learns to do things has to accept society's way of doing them. It is not so obvious, however, that the paradigmatic relation between the individual and society is a coercive one. This is an idea which is plausible only because feminists conflate the notions of authority and power.

Now, while the notion of power clearly does involve the possibility of coercion, the relation of the individual to authority is an internal one. This point is related to something I have been drawing on throughout this discussion, namely, Wittgenstein's perception that the possibility of meaningful behaviour presupposes the notion of following a rule. The possibility of there being a correct way of doing things, and of what we do being intelligible to others, necessarily involves reference to an established way of doing things, and this means that to participate in rule-governed activities is to accept authority. This relation between an established way of doing things and the notion of authority is clearly shown by Winch, who points out in 'Authority':

When we use words in the right way we do not think of ourselves as bowing to the dictates of an alien will. No, but then I want to say that to submit to authority (as opposed to being subjected to power) is not to be subject to an alien will. What one does is directed rather by the idea of the right way of doing things in connexion with the activity one is performing; and the authoritative character of an individual's will derives from its connexion with that idea of a right way of doing things. (p. 229)

This means that in the case of the individual who learns that a particular piece of behaviour is appropriate in certain circumstances or that a word has a certain meaning, what we have is a matter of *understanding*, something which is totally different from the kind of cleverness an animal might show by mechanically adapting its behaviour to avoid maltreatment. Feminists are blind to this distinction. According to an account like Winch's, the acceptance of at least some rules, and therefore of authority, is a necessary condition of our being able to make any sense of our lives at all. And an important corollary to this is that the eschewing of *all* rules — the claim, as Shulamith Firestone puts it, that a feminist revolution would result in 'an abolition of the cultural categories themselves, a mutual cancellation — a matter—antimatter explosion, ending with a poof! culture itself' (*The Dialectic of Sex*, p. 182) — would result not in an 'androgynous culture' (whatever that might be) but in the destruction of anything that might intelligibly be called a *human* life, a life in which human beings interact with each other.

Clearly, not all authority is legitimate, and not all consent to powers above is genuinely given, but it does not follow from this that all submission to authority threatens a person's autonomy. Whether we count something as the exercise of power rather than authority will depend not on some easy reference to a force outside the individual but on close and difficult discussion of the cases in question: we will consider the criteria that determine what counts as an exercise of authority, whether these have been violated and, if so, to what degree, any peculiar features of the situation which ought to be taken into account and so on, so that what may look like a case of external constraint and power in one situation may well seem like nothing of the sort in another.

Feminists, in their vehement criticism of the family, for instance, point out that it does not always create a haven of security and peace for its members. They argue, sometimes justifiably, that there is often a pretence of love where no real affection is felt and that parents all too frequently confuse their own interests with those of their children. Talk of discipline, for example, can all too often be an excuse for bending the freedom of wife and children to the husband's own interests. Duty or loyalty to parents may mean simply the relinquishing of all individual responsibility, conscience and initiative by the children. And from the point of view of education, the notion of a correct way of doing things often leaves no room for creative, unconventional thought and behaviour. Moreover, feminists tend to see all this as symptomatic of the more general dominance of patriarchy: it spreads its tentacles not only over women but over children as well. Refusing to be fooled by the idea that children need adults to take care of them, Firestone, for example, contends: 'By now people have forgotten what history has proven: that "raising" a child is tantamount to retarding his development. The best way to raise a child is to LAY OFF.' (*The Dialectic of Sex*, p. 90) And when she writes 'LAY OFF', she means, quite literally, that once a child is physically independent, he should be given the same freedom and independence as an adult, being answerable to no one except himself. Socialization and education, she urges, are nothing but disguises for the systematic oppression of children. Authority over children is always a case of the exertion of power.

In Firestone's view, the main, and perhaps the only, legitimate reason why a child needs the care of adults is its physical dependence. Once it is physically independent and capable of work — which could, of course, be at a much younger age than is the case in our society — it should be freed from the restraints of adult control, for fundamental to her argument is a conception of a child as nothing more than a physically immature creature, whose physical welfare is our sole responsibility.

However, what feminists like Firestone miss is that, unlike an animal, a child is not simply an immature creature but a human being who comes into a world which is already shaped by traditions and a culture and is still changing continuously. In order to live in the world, the child has to learn its ways, for better or for worse, in preparation for adulthood. What the world is like, the traditions and the culture into which he has been born, he can learn only from adults; and this precisely because they are older than he. The notion that the relation between adults and children should be based on equality is inappropriate because they do not and cannot stand on equal terms. The weakness of the child comes not only from his physical dependence but also from the fact that as a newcomer into the world, ignorant of its ways, he is not yet in a position to survive at all, let alone compete effectively. The authority that adults assume over children is a consequence — and, of course, this may be abused — of their responsibility to see to it that their children emerge well prepared from the temporary stage of childhood into adulthood. What exactly they are to be prepared for may well provoke heated discussion, but what cannot be in dispute is that they do need guidance and education of some kind. As Hannah Arendt points out in 'The Crisis in Education':

The child shares the state of becoming with all living things; in respect to life and its development, the child is a human being in process of becoming, just as a kitten is a cat in process of becoming. But the child is new only in relation to a world that was there before him, that will continue after his death, and in which he is to spend his life. If the child were not a newcomer in this human world but simply a not yet finished living creature, education would be just a function of life and would need to consist in nothing save that concern for the sustenance of life and that training and practice in living that all animals assume in respect to their young. (p. 185)

Therefore, she goes on to remark,

Insofar as the child is not yet acquainted with the world, he must be gradually introduced to it; insofar as he is new, care must be taken that this new thing comes to fruition in relation to the world as it is. In any case, however, the educators here stand in relation to the young as representatives of a world for which they must assume responsibility although they themselves did not make it, and even though they may, secretly or openly, wish it were other than it is. This responsibility is not arbitrarily imposed upon educators; it is implicit in the fact that the young are introduced by adults into a continuously changing world. Anyone who refuses to assume joint responsibility for the world should not have children and must not be allowed to take part in educating them.

In education this responsibility for the world takes the form of authority. The authority of the educator and the qualifications of the teacher are not the same thing. Although a measure of qualification is indispensable for authority, the highest possible qualification can never by itself beget authority. The teacher's qualification consists in knowing the world and being able to instruct others about it, but his authority rests on his assumption of responsibility for that world. *Vis-à-vis* the child it is as though he were a representative of all adult inhabitants, pointing out the details and saying to the child: This is our world. (p. 189)

Given the fact that the child is a newcomer into the world, the so-called rejection of power over children by feminists would not give them a better chance for self-expression; instead, the growth of the child would be stunted. However, as feminists insist that responsibility for children must be diffused through society as a whole, it may be that they are actually quite clear that they no longer wish to have authority over their children, thereby relinquishing responsibility for them. That such relinquishment of responsibility should be thought highly beneficial to children is crucial to feminism, for the premise on which women's liberation ultimately depends is the liberation of women from child-bearing and child-rearing. (I shall return to this point in chapter 6.) The plausibility of this claim depends on seeing authority as power, a conflation which leaves no space for the central role of the notion of responsibility in an adult's relations with children. This is quite explicit in the following remark made by Firestone in *The Dialectic of Sex*:

Most of child-*rearing* . . . has to do with the maintaining of power relations, forced internalization of family values, and many other ego concerns that war with the happiness of the individual child. This repressive socialization process would not be necessary in a society in which the interests of the individual coincided with those of the larger society. Any child-rearing responsibility left would be diffused to include men and other children equally with women. In addition, new methods of instant communication would lessen the child's reliance on even this egalitarian primary unit. (pp. 221−2)

Now, the difficulty of educating a child so that one contributes to the growth not of an automaton that simply obeys the rules but of a being who becomes genuinely acquainted with what has gone before him but does not become stifled by that past, a being who learns that the possibility of making sense to others and of communicating with them presupposes the acceptance of rules and tradition, is a problem that has always plagued educational theorists. Feminists assume, rather simplistically, that such difficulties can be avoided by denying the existence of one horn of the dilemma, namely, the need for rules and for education at all. Their justification seems to be based on the view that the past, in the form of rules, tradition and culture (representing, as they do, a limit to our freedom), is therefore necessarily oppressive. I have already pointed out what I take to be wrong with this view. In addition, they do not face the real difficulty here, the tension between the twofold task with which parents and educators are faced, the recognition of which need lead one neither to 'lay off' children nor to exercise an oppressive hold over them.

One way of understanding this duality is to see that a person in a position of authority is not the same as one in a position of power: the former may allow and encourage freedom on the part of his subjects without having his authority threatened, whereas this possibility is closed to someone in a position of power. That is to say, a profound respect for the freedom of the child may be wholly compatible with, and central to, the task that an educator sets himself. And, interestingly, the feeling that there may be something restricting in the education of children also invites a view of education that appears to resemble Firestone's and yet is radically different. This is apparent in Rousseau's conception of the relation between tutor and pupil. Of his method of education, Rousseau says in *Emile*:

Young teacher, I am setting before you a difficult task, the art of controlling without precepts, and doing everything without doing anything at all. This art is, I confess, beyond your years, it is not calculated to display your talents nor to make your value known to your scholar's parents; but it is the only road to success. (p. 84)

In another place he writes:

The education of the earliest years should be merely negative. It consists, not in teaching virtue or truth, but in preserving the heart from vice and from the spirit of error. If only you could let well alone, and get others to follow your example . . . [i]n your hands, [your pupil] would soon become the wisest of men; by doing nothing to begin with you would end with a prodigy of education. (pp. 57–8)

Yet for all this emphasis on doing nothing and on negative education, Rousseau, the tutor, is so totally engaged in the task of educating his pupil that this leaves little time for anything else in his life. A close reading of *Emile* reveals that Rousseau's main difficulty is to do everything but to give his pupil — not the reader — the impression that he does nothing. The emphasis on negative education does not liberate him from his awesome responsibility but only focuses on the problematic relationship between power and authority, of which he is so acutely aware. For one of the difficult tasks that Rousseau sets himself is to let his pupil 'think he is master while you are really master' (p. 84), thereby preserving the freedom of the child through strict, but careful, discipline. He says of his method, 'The spirit of these rules is to give children more real liberty and less power, to let them do more for themselves and demand less of others. . . .' (p. 35) According to Firestone's account, Rousseau's method of education must seem utterly paradoxical — one moment emphasizing freedom and the next moment emphasizing the need for rules. Yet what he says need not be regarded in this way if the sorts of distinctions between authority and power to which I have been drawing attention are heeded.

Hence when a man treats his wife as if she were his child, treats her as if only he could know what is best for her (think of Ibsen's *A Doll's House*), then we do have a case of external constraint and power; and what makes it such is the fact that a woman is not a child. Indeed, feminists are so confused about where their oppression lies that they actually see women's liberation as closely related to children's liberation. Nevertheless, it is precisely because the distinction between power and authority is crucial to the discussion that Firestone's following blueprint for children's liberation can be nothing but ridiculous. She argues in *The Dialectic of Sex* that women must not forsake the need of children to be liberated, even though

many women are sick and tired of being lumped together with children: that they are no more our charge and responsibility than anyone else's will be an assumption crucial to our revolutionary demands. It is only that we have developed, in our long period of related sufferings, a certain compassion and understanding for them that there is no reason to lose now; we know where they're at, what they're experiencing, because we, too, are still undergoing the same kind of oppressions. (p. 102)

This discussion of power and authority has been introduced in order to illustrate what is wrong with the way in which feminists view the relation between the individual and society. I want to show now that there are further misconceptions which play an important part in making what they say about roles and socialization implausible.

A central question for feminists is how far a woman or a man can be treated both as a member of a particular sex and as a person in his or her own right. One aim of liberation politics is to adapt society to the point where it allows individuals untrammelled freedom of self-expression, so that everyone can interact on a personal basis. On further inquiry, what this amounts to is a declaration, among other things, that women and children should be able to 'do whatever they wish to do sexually. There will no longer be any reason *not* to . . . . in our new society, humanity could finally revert to its natural polymorphous sexuality — all forms of sexuality would be allowed and indulged.' (*The Dialectic of Sex*, p. 195) What is significant here is the idea of freedom as activity that is totally unlicensed and free from any limits or constraints, moral, social or otherwise. But, as we have already seen, the suggestion that man loses his individuality and freedom by virtue of becoming a member of society fails to take into account the fact that such notions as freedom and individuality already presuppose a certain form of group life in which they play a role. To regard freedom, for example, as valuable is already to be part of a form of life of which traditions of democracy and rights constitute an integral part. Further, as already pointed out, to the extent that language and thinking are part of the natural history of human beings, society, with its public realm of rules and standards, is a *sine qua non* of human life. For similar reasons the existence of role-typing is an integral feature of any society, as we shall see.

The existence of language, Wittgenstein points out, presupposes that there should be agreement in our reactions. If we differed in our reactions, we could not speak. When I look up at the blue sky and say, 'What a fine day!' I do not wonder whether you will have the same visual impression as I. It is because we agree in our reactions that it is possible for me to tell you something and for you to teach me something. 'If language is to be a means of communication, there must be agreement not only in definitions but also (queer as this may sound) in judgements.' (*Philosophical Investigations*, para. 242) In other words, the possibility of speech and action presupposes a symmetry between the self and others, the commonality of men.

In sociological idiom, it might be said that the structure of a social role emphasizes the individual in so far as he is on a level with others. In positive terms, it might be said that the wearing of a common uniform (say) is intended not so much to deny the individuality of the wearers as perhaps to emphasize the aims or ideals that they share. That is to say, from one point of view, the generality of social roles serves to remind us of the common bases that form the foundation of our behaviour and the behaviour of others.[6] Consequently a society in which roles were eschewed would be a society in which men, having denied their commonality with each other, would regard each other as totally alien and foreign.

Nevertheless, we are also distinct and unique. This fact too has to be presupposed in any account of speech and action, for without it, speech and action would be unnecessary, as Hannah Arendt points out in *The Human Condition:*

Human plurality, the basic condition of both action and speech, has the twofold character of equality and distinction. If men were not equal, they could neither understand each other and those who came before them nor plan for the future and foresee the needs of those who will come after them. If men were not distinct, each human being distinguished from any other who is, was, or will ever be, they would need neither speech nor action to make themselves understood. Signs and sounds to communicate immediate, identical needs and wants would be enough. (pp. 175−6)[7]

This means that one shows one's individuality not by eschewing roles but by being the kind of woman or man one is. Of course role-typing should not necessarily be immune from criticism. Indeed, one

---

[6] This conception of social role is interestingly developed in Maurice Natanson, *The Journeying Self.*

[7] For further discussion of the asymmetry between the self and others, see also J. R. Jones, 'How do I know who I am?', who gives a penetrating elucidation of Wittgenstein's remarks on solipsism in the *Tractatus.*

of the most important things that feminists have demonstrated in their rejection of many feminine roles is, that such roles have become so ossified, so exploited by the media, so constrained by the kind of society in which we live, that they fail any longer to provide channels for the proper expression of individuality and idiosyncracy. To the extent that feminists argue that roles can sustain greater fluidity and flexibility than is realized, I think they are right. However, the promotion of fluidity and flexibility should not be taken to imply that anything will do and that the notion of a role can be made redundant. To do that, as we have seen, would be tantamount to denying the commonality of all human beings.

What needs pointing out is the dual aspect of society: on the one hand, the fact of our being in society enables us to talk of human beings and a human life at all, and yet, on the other, the force of society may be such that people experience it as restricting and oppressive in all sorts of ways. By this token, much of what feminists have to say about roles and the way in which society coerces the individual is a political thesis and cannot easily be transposed into an epistemological one, as many feminists seem to do, albeit unknowingly. Thus, while it is intelligible for people to discuss the nature of the state, what sort of society they want, what they dislike about their culture and so on, it can never make sense to talk of the abolition of society or the abolition of all institutions. This point, of course, calls into question the idea that social institutions, whichever they may be, are always functions of class struggle or sex-class struggle. It is for this reason that it is fallacious to think of socialization as a process only of indoctrination and depersonalization.

The reason for emphasizing that notions like authority and socialization entail quite specific relations between individuals and society is to show that such relations cannot be construed in functional terms.[8] Feminists are able to give a plausible account of sexism as a sex-class struggle only because they construe institutions in functional terms, in terms of some preconceived general hypothesis rather than on their own terms.

[8] That is to say, in terms of a quasi-causal relation.

From the above account of the relation between society and the individual it should be clear that our notions are closely related to one another; our notion of femininity is intertwined with the way in which we think about all sorts of other things. But this fact need not compel us to agree unthinkingly with the feminist slogan 'The personal is political.' Recognition of the fact that the various phenomena of human life are logically interrelated — although, let it be said again, this is not to say that all phenomena of human life are functions of economics or sex divisions — does mean that one issue cannot be dealt with in isolation from another. Moreover, it means that the temptation to want persistently to give structural priority to any one factor of social life is one that must be resisted. Failure to appreciate this point is evident in many of the functional accounts that feminists give of institutions.

Firestone, for example, states that marriage, along with the family, has become defunct because 'it is no longer necessary or most effective as the basic social unit for reproduction/production.' (*The Dialectic of Sex*, p. 206) The reason why marriage still presents itself as a possibility for many people is that it is able to reinforce male hegemony. It upholds the sex-class division. However, she goes on to argue, since it is now possible to reproduce artificially, the family, along with the child-bearing and child-rearing roles of women, is an archaic institution:

The birth of children to a unit which disbanded or recomposed as soon as children were physically independent, one that was meant to serve immediate needs rather than to pass on power and privilege . . . would eliminate the psychology of power, sexual repression, and cultural sublimation. Family chauvinism, class privilege based on birth, would wither away. The blood tie of the mother to the child would eventually be severed — if male jealousy of 'creative' childbirth actually exists, we shall soon have the means to create life independently of sex — so that pregnancy, now freely acknowledged as clumsy, inefficient, and painful, would be indulged in, if at all, only as a tongue-in-cheek archaism, just as already women today wear virginal white to their weddings. (p. 224)

The trouble with construing the relation in this way is that it makes it look as though questions about the nature of the family were straightforward factual or technical ones, whereas in fact what someone thinks about the family is going to depend, more than anything else, on which things are important to him in life, what his values are. People care about their children or their parents not because they think they owe it to society, nor because it happens to be the most economic way of taking care of the young and the infirm, nor because the family as an institution transmits class privileges. They simply do it — although, of course, the 'naturalness' of what they are doing is a product of its relation to many other things they take for granted but whose relation to the family as an institution is often unclear. And this lack of clarity may be the result not of insufficient thought or analysis but of the multifarious and complex reasons why family life is important to them.

The fact that the family as an institution is disintegrating may be indicative of a serious crisis in society, but the nature of this crisis cannot be understood in terms of the supposed threat that it poses to male supremacy. This is because human institutions are not *designed* to fulfil certain purposes. They come about for a multitude of reasons in a constellation of circumstances that are quite different from the functions for which an artefact may be devised. Difficulties encountered in human institutions are never like those posed by technology.

For example, people may find steam engines inefficient and wasteful and may decide that diesel locomotives are better. But this decision is possible because the criteria that determine what counts as efficient and what the function of a locomotive is are well defined. In such circumstances it would make sense to account for the obsolescence of steam engines by saying they had become defunct in the light of the advantages of diesels. Someone might disagree from an aesthetic point of view: he might prefer the chugging motion of a steam engine and its friendly puffing as it goes along. He realizes, however, that such considerations are totally irrelevant and indulges his nostalgia by joining a hobby society to keep steam engines going, archaic though they may be; and if asked about diesel engines, there would be no contradiction in his maintaining that the automatic diesels of today are certainly an advance.

But no woman could say that artificial reproduction constitutes an advance and yet still wish to conceive and bear children herself. It would not be nostalgia for things of the past that would constitute her resistance, as Firestone seems to think; it would be connected with a sense that something of value had been lost, and a moral judgement would be passed on the new state of affairs.

Firestone, along with most feminists (see, for example, Gould, 'The Woman Question', quoted on p. 7 above), thinks of reproduction as analogous to the production and manufacturing of goods. She presumes that procreation has a clearly defined function: to provide new members for society, and artificial reproduction is a more efficient, a simpler, a more convenient way of achieving this end. This is a grotesque thought because an act of procreation is not comparable with the manufacture of artefacts. A woman who has had a miscarriage or a stillborn baby feels *grief*, not disappointment at having failed to produce a desired object. If a potter breaks a vase that she has just made, she sees quite clearly that there is no point in crying over spilt milk and promptly begins to make another, whereas the immediate reaction of a woman whose baby is stillborn is not to say, 'Never mind, I'll try again.'

To people who have lost a newborn child through death, the child existed. It was carried for nine months, plans were made for its future, clothes and presents were bought, and labour was gone through to bring the child into the world. That it lived and died at the same time doesn't alter the fact of its existence and its place in your heart and memory — that of the first-born, or of the sister or brother who died. For other people there are no memories, no recollections to be made about the dead person and often, because they didn't know your child as you did, there seems to be a suggestion — hurtful and distressing to you — that the child didn't really exist: 'You can have another one' or 'You're lucky you've already got one.' Of course you can, if you wish, have another child, but it will be the one born after the one that died and the dead one remains for most people a part of the same family. (Beels, *The Childbirth Book*, p. 229)

Firestone is able to talk as she does because she sees the problems she is discussing — problems associated with family relations, sexual tensions, how to bring up one's children — as a series of technical problems, in which the relationship between the individual and society is a purely functional one; we presumably all know where we are going or want to go, and the only difficulty is the technical expertise necessary to achieve our ends. And it is precisely in so far as such writers regard the determined attempt by men to reinforce male hegemony as the only reason for the present resistance to this way of thinking about social problems that feminism, far from being either radical or revolutionary, reveals itself to be perhaps the most articulate expression of the philosophy of a society in which human life is continually trivialized and cheapened for the sake of extraneous, abstract aims.

In conclusion, it might be said that the functionalist account that feminists give of social life has blinded them to the enormous opportunities open to people to make sense of their lives. They stipulate what *the* road to a successful life is and fail to see that differences over this issue are not empirically inadequate but depend ultimately on questions of value, which are irreducible. This tendency is quite explicit in, for example, Julia Annas's contention, in 'Mill and the Subjection of Women', that

liberation will lead to greater happiness for women. . . . Asian women do not mind being in purdah, and find the thought of going about freely shocking, but this does not mean that they should not be liberated from seclusion, or that they would not appreciate freedom once they had it; and the same holds for European women who cannot appreciate why it is important for them to be financially independent. (p. 193)

This may be true, but equally it may not. It is imperative to see that lack of appreciation here may have nothing to do with ignorance, with something the woman has never thought of.[9] In this connection

[9] For instance, it is worth considering that the purdah of Asian women may be intended not so much to oppress them as to serve as a physical reminder of the

think, for example, of Socrates' discussion with Callicles in the *Gorgias* about the question of whether it is better to suffer evil than to do evil: Callicles fails to see that Socrates is aware of the power, wealth and pride that would be conferred by a certain sort of life, but these things are of no importance to him beside his desire to lead a good life. Likewise, a woman's lack of appreciation of the need for financial independence may be related to certain features of her life or to certain beliefs in such a way that economic dependence could not be a liberating force for her. To recognize this, however, it is necessary to see that not all relations of dependence are founded on impotence or on economic weakness. And the inevitable failure of feminists to recognize this is connected with further difficulties in the way in which they construe our notion of femininity as a social fact.

---

sacredness of the private sphere, thought to be the proper sphere of women. In a different but perhaps related context, Hannah Arendt remarks (she is speaking of Ancient Greece) that the seclusion of women is connected with this fact because

> The sacredness of this privacy [of private property] was like the sacredness of the hidden, namely, of birth and death, the beginning and end of the mortals who, like all living creatures, grow out of and return to the darkness of the underworld. The non-privative trait of the household realm originally lay in its being the realm of birth and death which must be hidden from the public realm because it harbors the things hidden from human eyes and impenetrable to human knowledge. It is hidden because man does not know where he comes from when he is born and where he goes when he dies. (*The Human Condition*, p. 62—3)

In a sense, the emancipation of women in our society goes hand in hand with a total loss of a sense of the mystery of birth and death. The idea that we have 'solved' these mysteries is an illusion. The truth of the matter is that we simply do not think of them, and when we are forced to, we tend to do everything possible to eliminate them from human life.

5

Nature and Convention I:
Rousseau on the Nature of Woman

It is a striking fact that many writers on the subject of women's rights take it as axiomatic that the undisputed difference between the sexes — that men beget and women give birth — is irrelevant to the question of what occupations the two sexes should follow and how they should be treated. It might be said that a feminist argument is almost by definition one that contends that this difference need never, and should never, be of any significance in our treatment of the sexes. As Juliet Mitchell puts it: 'Biological differences between men and women obviously exist but it is not these that are the concern of feminists.' ('Women and Equality', p. 379)

Feminists simply regard it as false to think that bodily functions like pregnancy and childbirth are *sui generis*. By contrast, they tend to regard them as being no different from bodily disorders such as heart attacks or appendicitis; and just as no one expects to have different occupational structures for those who have undergone appendectomies, so it is an expression of mere cultural prejudice to think that pregnancy and childbirth should limit a woman's sphere of activity. Indeed, it is more than prejudice: it serves to rationalize the oppression of women as sex objects by men. That is to say, women are confined to the limits of the domestic sphere not because it is a given fact of nature that they — as opposed to their husbands or other members of the community — have a special responsibility in relation to the children they have borne, but simply in order that men may remain dominant and may pursue their selfish interests uncontested. This is why, as we saw in chapter 4, feminists claim that sex roles are based on convention and not on facts of nature.

This argument is unsatisfactory, however. We cannot begin to understand a particular convention without referring to the fact of nature of which it aims to make sense. It is important to note that despite the obvious fact that human life is everywhere bounded by the immutable exigencies of birth and sex, feminists assert, without argument, that our sex conventions are not directly related to these facts at all. We are invited to imagine that these conventions are trumped up simply for the benefit of men, and that the nature of birth and sex is irrelevant to feminist discussion. This is extraordinary, for it is eminently natural that where we should look first in an attempt to understand sexual conventions is the inescapable human realities of which they aim to make sense.

Feminists resist this, first because an emphasis on natural facts or on biology seems to suggest that women are *conditioned* by biology and, secondly, because their conception of human life constitutes a profound revolt against the fact that to be human is to be limited by certain natural conditions. I shall deal with these two issues separately in this chapter and the next.

The recognition that sex roles differ culturally has led feminists to see that sex differences cannot be understood simply in biological terms. And they contend that the implication of this, as we noted above, is that our sex roles are therefore quite arbitrary. This is how Carol Gould puts it in 'The Woman Question':

In claiming that significant differences between men and women are thoroughly historical, social and cultural, I am indeed denying that the difference is fundamentally or significantly biological. That there *are* biological differences between men and women is obviously true. The point is that there are infinitely many differences among individuals, any of which is logically an equal candidate for making group distinctions among humans . . . Which ones have been selected [for importance] is a function of the historical, social and cultural role which has been assigned to the characteristic in question. Thus, in denying that the biological difference is an essential or fundamental difference, I am asserting . . . that the gender distinction between men and women is . . . not a given fact of nature. (pp. 39—40n.)

Gould is right to point out that our conceptions of sex differences take their shape from the form of life in which they play a role. But while the point of describing something as a convention is to see that things could be otherwise, and that how we perceive them is always relative to our interests, problems, and purposes, this does not mean that our actions and institutions are therefore arbitrary. That something is a convention should not blind us to the fact that it may nevertheless be rooted in nature and not in mere opinion. We do, of course, have some freedom of choice regarding conventions, in the sense that we can reject or modify them at will, but it is important to remember that the possibility of any choice presupposes a framework within which there are intelligible alternatives. Thus it would be appropriate to remark here, as did Wittgenstein in a different context, 'Then there is something arbitrary about this system? Yes and no. It is akin both to what is arbitrary and to what is non-arbitrary.' (*Zettel*, para. 358)

When talking about gender distinctions, this framework is provided by the undisputed biological differences between the sexes. That is to say, the sense we give to the fact that women menstruate, for example, is arbitrary to the extent that the way we regard such a fact is not absolutely conditioned by biology. The biological fact alone cannot tell us whether to regard a menstruating woman as unclean and possessed of special powers to do harm on the one hand, or as indicative of the potential such a woman has to procreate on the other. That choice will depend on the sort of society in which we live. Yet such a question can present itself to us only because we are faced with the given fact of nature that women do menstruate. Hence whatever other prejudices may embroider the significance we give to this, it cannot be considered a *cultural* prejudice not to give young boys at puberty instruction in this matter: no convention can change the fact that *they* will not menstruate.

Thus a man who feels a desire to bear children — he is otherwise quite normal — will not agitate for equal rights but will be more inclined to wonder whether he is in the right body, quite literally. The tragic plight of a trans-sexual (as described, for instance, in Jan Morris's book *Conundrum*) moves us not to indignation and anger but, more likely, to pity and compassion because we naturally see that this sort of case is different from that of a disadvantaged group of people whose misery is clearly attributable to social inequities, a point already evident from the opening sentence of the book: 'I was three or perhaps four years old when I realized that I had been born into the wrong body and should really be a girl.' And while it may be that the problems of trans-sexuals have not been accorded the seriousness they deserve, it would be wrong to think that the failure to deal with such a problem is due to lack of political imagination. This is because we are most likely to find ourselves overwhelmed and perplexed, with no idea of how a satisfactory solution can be found in such cases.

Feminists insist that everything we do or say is based on convention. Thus, for example, to find certain sexual deviances abnormal is to be guilty of conservativism and poor anthropological imagination. They insist that such differences are not tolerated only because we are unjustifiably bound by our cultural categories. But would it be really kind and thoughtful to say to someone like Jan Morris that it is a mere convention to think that only women should experience the desire to have children and to dress up in women's clothing — the implication being that this problem is similar to that of the little boy who refuses to wear a pink jumper for fear of being ridiculed by his classmates? Surely it would not. Indeed, the whole thrust of Morris's description of her feelings is to show that what she was facing was not at all akin to a neurosis, and that her real difficulty was to impress upon psychiatrists that she wished to be taken literally when she asserted that she had been made in the wrong body and that her feelings were not projections of male inadequacy, for instance. Of course, it is not surprising that most of the psychiatrists reacted with scepticism and disbelief because there is something profoundly disturbing in being presented with a case of this sort. At any rate, the deep disquietude we feel about trans-sexuality rests not on a failure to be more tolerant but on the feeling that such phenomena destroy the sense we are able to make of the facts of nature on which our lives are based. To think that the obvious differences between the sexes are unimportant, as feminists do, would mean that such disquietude would have to be regarded as irrational and, further, that Morris was mistaken in thinking that she needed a sex change.

The suggestion that biological facts matter and affect the nature of the relations between the sexes should not be seen as an attempt to settle any questions: it only raises them. It certainly does not mean that our biological state conditions our lives absolutely. But it does mean that in so far as human beings are embodied — and this is related to the point made in chapter 1 that, in a certain sense, man is very much an animal — our sexual conventions cannot be understood adequately if, in discussing them, we sever them from the obvious differences between the sexes of which they aim to make sense.

The question of how to conceive of the relation between a social convention and a biological fact is a difficult one. Already, in criticizing the views of both feminists and Freudian theorists on this issue, we saw that the relation of biology to a person's life cannot be thought of in causal terms, and, contrary to the arguments of feminists, that the absence of a law-like relation between sex and our sexual conventions does not mean that those conventions are arbitrary. However, despite the existence of considerable variations in the ways in which people at different periods and in different cultures have thought about sex, it is imperative to see that these varying conventions have nevertheless related to two immutable facts of human life: birth and sexual relations. To avoid misunderstanding, I do not want to say — as do feminists — that the absence of a causal relation between biological facts and behaviour means that the general natural or biological realities of human life are irrelevant to this discussion. Rather, the point is that if we want to understand how such facts affect our lives, what we require is not a study in biochemistry but an account of the internal relations between our sexual conventions and the natural facts of which they aim to make sense. Indeed, much of the difficulty with the way in which feminists think of our notions of femininity stems, crucially, from the fact that they fail to relate our beliefs about sex differences to the biological realities of the fact that human life begins with *birth* and that, for women, sex is inextricably bound up with procreation.

Kate Millett is right in thinking that many of the studies of sex and temperament are unsatisfactory (see above, p. 59). But what these studies reveal as insecure is not the incontrovertible difference between the sexes — that men beget and women give birth — on which sex behaviour is based, but the attempt to discover a psycho-physiological parallelism between physical states and behaviour, a notion which philosophers have rendered wholly disreputable. What we need to see is that the obvious, undisputed differences between the sexes have a fundamental role to play in this discussion, for the ways in which they affect our lives cannot be adequately accounted for by culture alone. We cannot hope to gain any understanding of our sexual conventions if we do not make an attempt seriously to relate them to the realities of birth and sex. In a different but not unrelated context, Peter Winch draws attention to the importance of this requirement:

the very conception of human life involves certain fundamental notions — which I shall call 'limiting notions' — which have an obvious ethical dimension, and which indeed in a sense determine the 'ethical space' within which the possibilities of good and evil in human life can be exercised. The notions . . . correspond closely to those which Vico made the foundation of his idea of natural law, on which he thought the possibility of understanding human history rested: birth, death, sexual relations. Their significance here is that they are inescapably involved in the life of all known human societies in a way which gives us the clue where to look if we are puzzled about the point of an alien system of institutions. The specific forms which these concepts take, the particular institutions in which they are expressed, vary very considerably from one society to another; but their central position within a society's institutions is and must be a constant factor. In trying to understand the life of an alien society, then, it will be of the utmost importance to be clear about the way in which these notions enter into it. (*Ethics and Action,* pp. 42–3)

And, of course, the same applies if we wish to understand the point of certain institutions in our own society.

It is for this reason that Rousseau, for instance, makes an

important contribution to the discussion on sex differences in *Emile*. He consciously comes to terms with the nature of the immutable facts of birth and sex and tries to relate these to our conceptions of sex differences. In this way his discussion touches the nerve of the problem: given that there are undisputed biological differences between the sexes, he shows how far a *biological* argument can be advanced to justify differential treatment of the sexes.

Of all the proposals put forward for the education of women, Rousseau's discussion in *Emile* must be one of the most infuriating accounts any feminist is likely to encounter, since he says that the education of women should be directed towards pleasing men. However, he has a further argument for the differential treatment of the sexes, which is the more interesting and also more relevant to his own concerns. The pivotal point on which Rousseau's discussion of sex differences turns is the traditional view that the lot of woman is to become a wife and mother. However, his argument with convention stops there. For where most writers see this as a reason for arguing against the education of women, Rousseau sees this difference as requiring a special sort of education for them.

He introduces his educational proposals for Sophie by maintaining, as do feminists, that apart from the biological consequences of sex, the sexes are the same: 'But for her sex, a woman is a man; she has the same organs, the same needs, the same faculties. The machine is the same in its construction; its parts, its working, and its appearance are similar. Regard it as you will, the difference is only in degree.' (p. 321) Nevertheless, he insists, it makes all the difference that a woman is a woman and that a man is a man because of the biological asymmetry in their sexual lives, a difference that manifests itself in the distinct part each plays in the sexual act itself and in the fact that it is the woman who has the procreative role. Sometimes Rousseau seems to suggest that this physical asymmetry demonstrates an asymmetry in the mental capacities of men and women, thus contradicting himself. However, for the most part — at any rate, this is all he needs to admit — his view seems to be that a different attitude or stance towards life is required of the sexes because of the dissimilar biological demands that will be made on them by sex. A young boy will hardly have to consider limits imposed on his working life by pregnancy and the need to suckle infants, whereas a girl needs to be made to face squarely the physical restrictions that pregnancy and children will impose on her possible range of activities — feminists have shown often enough that there is little likelihood that she will do so otherwise — and to think of her life in relation to these. Failure to do so will inevitably lead to frustration and disappointment as she finds her freedom curtailed by the needs of her infant and will leave her ill-equipped to deal with her maternal role.

In short, Rousseau relates the different education of Emile and Sophie to the peculiar problems and purposes that their sexual roles will generate when they are adults. The choice we have to face is not *whether* to educate girls but *how* to do so. Thus Rousseau says:

The consequences of sex are wholly unlike for man and woman. The male is only a male now and again, the female is always a female, or at least all her youth; everything reminds her of her sex; the performance of her functions requires a special constitution. She needs care during pregnancy and freedom from work when her child is born; she must have a quiet, easy life while she nurses her children; their education calls for patience and gentleness, for a zeal and love which nothing can dismay; she forms a bond between the father and child, she alone can win the father's love for his children and convince him that they are indeed his own. What loving care is required to preserve a united family! And there should be no question of virtue in all this, it must be a labour of love, without which the human race would be doomed to extinction.

The mutual duties of the two sexes are not, and cannot be, equally binding on both. Women do wrong to complain of the inequality of man-made laws; this inequality is not of man's making, or at any rate it is not the result of mere prejudice, but of reason. (p. 324)

Rousseau's argument rests, then, on the fact that it is because of her procreative role that woman does not stand in the same relation to life as man. His contention is that women are not always free to engage in the same activities as men because of the limits imposed upon them by their biological constitution — by biological facts like pregnancy, parturition, lactation. If we take stock of how these factors affect their lives, it should come as no surprise that the difference between men and women is not like the difference between male and female watchdogs, as Plato thought.

At a primitive, biological level, Rousseau stresses, being a mother is a mode of being in the world that is radically different from being childless or being a man. At this primitive level the mother stands, in contrast to the father and to others, in a unique and individual relation to the new-born infant. It is she who has carried him for nine months, felt him alive and kicking in her womb, experienced her breasts swell in preparation for the milk that is to nourish him until he is physically mature enough for other food; it is she who has given birth to him in agonizing pain. And it is because of these *biological* givens that she stands in a privileged position as regards the needs of the infant. Further, if her feelings for the child are to develop into ones of positive affection rather than resentment (say), one thing she will have to accept, Rousseau would remind us, is the infant's passive and complete dependence on her, with all the limitations and restrictions such dependence will inevitably impose upon her life and upon her range of activities. Rousseau is drawing attention to the fact that the needs of babies make very real demands on their mothers. Given the physical realities of motherhood, it is not surprising that many women devote this period of their lives to little else. The possibility of going out to work does not liberate them; it simply doubles their burden.

Moreover, in so far as two of the new-born infant's most pressing demands are immediate, physical, sensual contact with one other human being and nourishment, it seems eminently natural, from a biological point of view, that this person should be the mother rather than the father because it is the mother who conceives the child, carries it, gives birth to it and suckles it. If men also had breasts, say, then there might be some grounds for complaint. Of course, the dependence of the infant on the mother in this way wanes as it matures physically; gradually it becomes ready for, and seeks, the attention of its father and others. It is with considerations of this sort in mind that in *Emile* Rousseau writes: 'When once it is proved that men and women are and ought to be unlike in constitution and in temperament, it follows that their education must be different.' (p. 326)

Now, many people have thought that women are especially good at mothering because of a natural bent or instinct. Tempting and attractive though this idea of a natural maternal instinct may be — if only because it sustains the naive belief that every mother will necessarily be a good one — it is fallacious. In his own time Rousseau himself was fully aware of the fact that the idea of a maternal instinct was not incontrovertible, for he had been struck by the irresponsible behaviour of some women towards their children; but whereas Mary Wollstonecraft, for instance, thought that such behaviour could be attributed to the fact that women were not educated according to the 'rules of pure reason' (*A Vindication of the Rights of Women*, p. 117) and were denied the privileges of a masculine education, Rousseau presents women with detailed instruction in the care of infants (see *Emile*, Book 1). In his favour it can be said that he realized that unless some instruction and experience in the care of infants, however informal, were received — details concerning the importance of breast-feeding, the treatment of common ailments, swaddling practices, bathing procedure and so on — no natural instincts would give the young mother any clue to what was required to satisfy the needs of her infant: she would find herself helpless. For all his emphasis on the natural, Rousseau leaves extraordinarily little to nature; the feminine virtues and skills, like those Emile has to learn, must be cultivated and nurtured if they are to be acquired. He does not suggest — and this is what he is facing up to — that there is an innate or natural capacity in women which will automatically settle for them the problems surrounding the facts and trials of birth, infancy and childhood. He sees quite clearly that human conventions, although based in nature, are not determined by it.

At this point it is worth adding that Rousseau's 'back to nature' argument does not indicate a rejection of education and discipline; it presents itself — among other things — as a standard against which to judge the senselessness of many social practices. The emphasis is on looking at what the concrete, individual case requires rather than blindly and lazily resorting to some abstract conception. Time and again his point seems to be that every society must be founded on the way men are. He accepts that this means that certain defects are inevitable, but any attempt to construct a just society that aims to evade these defects by ignoring what men are like is doomed to failure. He is not saying, therefore, that human *nature* conditions the fabric of a society: only that there are certain inexorable facts about human life which it is wise to take into account. The importance of these is missed by feminists.

Firestone, for example, argues in *The Dialectic of Sex* that orphaned children in our society suffer badly because the natural love for children in society is unequally distributed between those who have parents and those who do not. The emphasis on rights as opposed to justice[1] in feminist discussion tends to make her think of love as having a fixed quantity — as is the case with goods like food and money — which must be shared out equally among the members of society: 'if *no one* had exclusive relationships with children, then *everyone* would be free for *all* children. The natural interest in children would be diffused over all children rather than narrowly concentrated on one's own.' (p. 197n.) But what Firestone misses is that concern about one's behaviour towards others presupposes certain conditions and surroundings in which notions of concern, affection and caring already have a place. If there really were no relations between people in society, other than the contractual ones of the civil sphere, it would be impossible for us to feel sympathy or affection for others. Instead we would regard others as a means to our own egotistical ends. Moreover, the significance of a contract would be debased if notions of rights and the demand for equality

---

[1] For some interesting remarks on the distinction between the notion of rights and the notion of justice, see Simone Weil's essay 'Human Personality'. She points out, for example: 'The notion of rights is linked with the notion of sharing out, of exchange, of measured quantity. It has a commercial flavour, essentially evocative of legal claims and arguments.' (p. 18)

lacked the background that made it possible for them to be accorded any seriousness. It is only because there are relations between people which are exclusive and particular in character — those between husbands and wives, between siblings, between parents and children, between friends — that we are able to make the judgements we do about the plight of orphaned children. Given different preoccupations, it is possible to imagine a society in which orphaned children were sold off as slaves or infanticide was regarded as the most obvious solution. Hence there is nothing 'visionary', to use Julia Annas's word,[2] about Firestone's conjecture concerning the results of abolishing exclusive relationships.

Feminists assert that the family is an institution which has served only to oppress women and children. But Firestone herself fails to show that her alternative to the family — a household based on a limited contract — wouild ensure that no one child would be favoured and that all children would be loved for their own sakes. What is clear from her description of the projected household is that she envisages an emotionally barren structure in which emotional attachments or commitments to others could not even be entered into intelligibly. Further, her description suggests a society in which love for children is wholly absent:

A group of ten or so consenting adults of varying ages could apply for a licence as a group in much the same way as a young couple today applies for a marriage licence. . . . The household licence would, however, apply only for a given period, perhaps seven to ten years, or whatever was decided on as the minimal time in which children needed a stable structure in which to grow up — but probably a much shorter period than we now imagine. If at the end of this period the group decided to stay together, it could always get a renewal. However, no single individual would be contracted to stay after this period, and perhaps some members of the unit might transfer out, or new members come in. Or, the unit could disband altogether. (ibid., pp. 215—16)

I agree that in that kind of society the distinction between children

[2] See Annas, 'Plato's *Republic* and Feminism', p. 319.

with parents and orphaned children would disappear, but only because all children would effectively be deprived of parents.

Feminists want every one to be treated the same, claiming that those distinctions that might justify our treating people differently ought to be destroyed. But in wanting everyone to be a mother to every child, for instance, Rousseau would argue, Firestone misses the significance of certain natural facts about human existence. She fails to understand how the natural facts of human existence play a central role in the structure of our ethical institutions.

Of course, the world might be a better place if a woman were capable of loving every child as her own. Yet, Rousseau would reply, it is natural and perfectly in order that she should feel greater affection for a child she has borne and cared for herself. This is inevitable, given the conditions of human life, because the peculiar nature of maternal love is defined by the primitive biological bond between mother and infant and, more especially, by the care and attention that she bestows upon it. The special love of a mother for her child is a product of their close physical intimacy, on which the baby is dependent if it is to stay alive and grow. This is why, for example, Rousseau discourages women from entrusting the care of their infants to others: 'If the voice of instinct is not strengthened by habit, it soon dies, the heart is still-born. From the outset we have strayed from the path of nature.' (*Emile*, p. 14) Thus he argues that breast-feeding is important because through such physical intimacy the emotional bond between mother and infant is nurtured and strengthened. And precisely because in her relations with her infant a mother has to do 'not with man, a hero, a demigod, but with a small, prattling soul, lost in a fragile and dependent body' (Beauvoir, *The Second Sex*, p. 492), he would argue that a rich, vital relationship between mother and infant receives sustenance from their immediate, sensuous, physical contact during breast-feeding.

It is also worth noting at this point that the importance of breast-feeding in the relationship between mother and infant is connected with the *natural* rhythms of the human body. The natural aspects of this relationship cannot be changed or destroyed without the risk of changing its very character. This is quite evident from the perceptive criticisms that Margaret Mead has made of modern hospital childbirth:

The failure of milk, the failure of the baby to nurse . . . are all natural enough in a setting where the new child is treated as if its health and well-being depended on the machine-like precision with which it is fed, and on what it is fed. The mother learns impatience with her milk, which is too rich or too weak, too much or too little, pouring through nipples that are inverted or sore or otherwise unobliging. She can turn with some relief to the bottle and the formula, the reliable rubber nipple with a hole that can be enlarged with a pin, the graduated bottle into which just the right formula, at just the right temperature can be measured. No recalcitrant, individual, unregulated human body here, to endanger her baby's gain in weight, the chief criterion of its healthful existence. . . . most American mothers reject their own bodies as a source of food for their children, and in accepting the mechanical perfection of a bottle, reaffirm to themselves, and in the way they handle their babies, that the baby too will be much better the more it learns to use the beautifully mechanical bottle . . . the more it accepts an external rhythm, and abandons its own peculiar rhythms that it brought into the world. For the primary learning experience that is the physical prototype of the sex relationship — a complementary relation between the body of the mother and the body of the child — is substituted a relationship between the child and an object, an object that imitates the breast, but which is not handled as either part of the mother or part of the baby. . . . At what age the child distinguishes the exact difference between a glass bottle and a rubber nipple . . . and a human breast we do not know, but the mother experiences the difference from the start, and her experience is available to the child, in her voice, in her hands, in the very tempo of her being. She is not giving the child herself; she is faithfully, efficiently, providing the child with a bottle, external to both of them, substituting for a direct relationship a relationship mediated by an object. (*Male and Female*, pp. 250–1)

Significantly, then, the 'strengthening of instinct by habit' nourishes the love between mother and child and explains why a mother automatically feels differently towards her own children. It explains too why the relationship between a child and its foster-mother may be deeper and richer than that between the child and its natural mother, whom it does not see. Finally it helps to explain why a society based on the isolated, nuclear family is incapable of meeting the needs of such children as orphans. The problem seldom arises in communities in which a child's vital relationships extend to others beyond his immediate kin (think of the extended family), with whom there is therefore a bond of affection comparable with that between him and his parents which will readily form the basis of a set of new relationships in the event of his parents' death.

In opposition to a position like Firestone's, Rousseau would have argued that a family structure such as the nuclear one is unhealthy precisely because it goes against nature. It wrongly assumes, for example, that a child's parents will always be there to care for it and ignores the fact that parents may die before their children are independent. Yet he would not have said that this fact about human life *in itself* can tell us what sort of family structure to adopt or what to do with orphaned children. The solution to these will depend on other considerations, which are not of a natural kind — notably on the wider political, economic and practical issues which are always relative to one's moral outlook and the purposes, interests and aims of the peculiar form of life in which one lives.[3] The salient point is that while natural facts do not determine our institutions in any absolute sense, we are likely to get into trouble sooner or later if the structure of our social institutions is such that it ignores, consciously or unconsciously, the passive givens of human existence.[4]

---

[3] It is important, therefore, that Rousseau's position should not be confused, for example, with the ethical naturalism once propounded by Philippa Foot and still influential among philosophers.

[4] Cf. the following remarks of Simone Weil on the reasons for the catastrophic state of our civilization:

> Never has the individual been so completely delivered up to a blind collectivity, and never have men been less capable, not only of subordinating their actions to thoughts, but even of thinking. Such terms as oppressors and oppressed, the idea of classes — all that sort of thing is near to losing all meaning, so obvious are the impotence and distress of all men in face of the social machine, which has become a machine for breaking hearts and crushing

I have dwelt at some length on the biological realities of birth, of the relation of the mother to her infant and of the helplessness and dependence of the human infant, in order to show that the differences in the child-rearing roles of men and women are fundamentally and significantly biological.[5] This point is connected too with my earlier claim that a judgement passed on a convention cannot claim to be fair if it ignores, among other things, the natural facts on which the convention is based. Hence Rousseau would say, against feminists, that a woman's sphere of activity is not limited, first and foremost, by male oppression but by the immediate, physical needs of the human infant. He would maintain it is difficult to see how a woman's life can be like a man's so long as women fall pregnant and human beings come into the world through birth.

It might well be argued that many writers are incapable of seeing

spirits, a machine for manufacturing irresponsibility, stupidity, corruption, slackness and, above all, dizziness. The reason for this painful state of affairs is perfectly clear. We are living in a world in which nothing is made to man's measure; there exists a monstrous discrepancy between man's body, man's mind and the things which at the present time constitute the elements of human existence: everything is disequilibrium, except perhaps for a few isolated patches of more primitive life; and the younger generation, who have grown and are growing up in it, inwardly reflect the chaos surrounding them more than do their elders. This disequilibrium is essentially a matter of quantity. Quantity is changed into quality, as Hegel said, and in particular a mere difference in quantity is sufficient to change what is human into what is inhuman. From the abstract point of view quantities are immaterial, since you can arbitrarily change the unit of measurement; but from the concrete point of view certain units of measurement are given and have hitherto remained invariable, such as the human body, human life, the year, the day, the average quickness of human thought. Present-day life is not organized on the scale of all these things; it has been transported into an altogether different order of magnitude, as though man were trying to raise it to the level of the forces of outside nature while neglecting to take his own nature into account. If we add that, to all appearances, the economic system has exhausted its constructive capacity and is beginning to function only by undermining little by little its own material foundations, we shall perceive in all its simplicity the veritable essence of the bottomless misery that forms the lot of the present generations. (*Oppression and Liberty*, p. 109)

[5] Also in order to counter the arguments of certain feminists: see, for example, Millett, *Sexual Politics,* p. 68; Gould, 'The Woman Question', p. 94.

anything but enforced subservience in the domestic role of women precisely because they fail to come to terms with the natural facts of birth and the link between sex and procreation for women. This is the problem, for example, with A. I. Melden's discussion of women's rights in his book *Rights and Persons*. Melden aims to say something about rights and sex differences without either relating his discussion to, or taking any heed of, the natural differences between the sexes, despite the fact that the main concern of his book seems to be to show that our concept of a person must be understood in relation to the concrete situations in which it is used. He never comes face to face with the fact that *female* persons are different in significant ways from male persons.

In a chapter entitled 'Rights, Personal Relations and the Family' Melden rightly claims that we cannot understand the nature of a right unless we look at the actual situations in which claims to a certain right are expressed. We will see that such utterances are addressed to persons with interests and concerns of many different kinds during the course of their interactions with one another. In contradiction to abstract, rationalist ethics, he emphasizes that this point is important because 'we are concerned here . . . with persons, not disembodied pure intelligences, who are engaged in the pursuit of their interests in ways that are intelligible and acceptable to us as moral agents' (p. 62). Hence although the aspect of agency is a feature essential to the existence of rights and obligations, this emphasis in itself makes it difficult to see how young children can have rights and also obligations to their parents. Traditional arguments try to make sense of this paradox by focusing attention on the future potential of children to be fully fledged agents. Melden rightly points out that this has to be accepted only if one forgets that our concept of a person is not of a pure intelligence but of a being continually changing from its first beginnings at birth, when his status as an agent is extremely limited, to adulthood; and that therefore 'rights and obligations are distributed among the members of a family as their lives are joined and the agency of each, in different and changing ways, supports the agencies of others' (p. 67). Thus 'what is essential to the existence of rights and obligations is the mutual understanding, which need not even be expressly formulated, that exists between them, of the crucial ways in which they are linked, as supporting agents, in their various lines of conduct' (p. 67). But we cannot even begin to realize that this is how we apply utterances of rights and obligations without exorcising the notion of a 'disembodied pure intelligence' from our concept of a person. To do this effectively we need, among other things,

in our conception of what it is to be a person, to bring that concept back to where it has its place in our practical discourse about persons. Our concept of a person applies to a being who is born helpless; completely dependent upon those who have prepared for its birth and who nurse and care for it; reciprocating the love and affection it receives from them as it is brought increasingly into the life of the family; learning first in this context and, later on, as its moral education progresses, in the wider community of which the family is only one small part, how within the limits imposed by concern with and respect for others, to conduct itself in various sorts of enterprises in many of which it counts on others for the success with which, as it grows in stature as a responsible agent, it pursues its affairs, first within the family circle and later with friends, acquaintances and strangers. (p. 66)

In such developing circumstances different considerations are relevant to the various obligations of child to parent, of brother to sister, of husband to wife and of parent to child. That is to say, the rights and obligations of husband and wife *vis-à-vis* each other will have to be understood in terms that are quite different from those that define the rights and obligations that parents owe to their children. The nature of the rights or obligations at stake cannot be understood outside the contexts in which they are raised.

Yet despite these important emendations to traditional discussions of rights, Melden goes on to assert, with feminists, that the domestic role of women is based on a violation of their rights. He contends:

The unjust restrictions imposed upon the endeavors of women is a violation of that right that they have to pursue the interests that go beyond those social roles to which they have been restricted by custom and tradition. . . . in this case there is a wide-ranging restriction or interference with those varying endeavors in which women do have an interest, which social taboos, customs and practices of various sorts have imposed upon women, thus impairing in these many ways and respects their very moral agency and subjecting them, as women have recently complained, to the treatment of them not as persons but often as sex objects — to bring children into the world, rear them, and to cater to the needs, at home, of their husbands. (pp. 176—7)

But the right to pursue one's interests is surely (and particularly according to Melden's account) not one that can exist without qualification. The endeavours of many women are certainly restricted by custom and tradition, but this restriction relates to the fact that women have babies and that babies make certain peculiar demands on their mothers and not on their fathers. Melden wishes his reader to accept — rightly — that the relation between parents and their children is a moral one: that is, that the blood bond places them in a relationship that is ethically fundamental. Consequently, Melden's argument here involves him in a contradiction. He fails to see that one cannot claim that the relationship between parents and children is a *moral* one if one asserts at the same time that in fulfilling her obligations to her children by providing for their needs in the form of nursing, cleaning, sewing, cooking, ironing, washing and so on, a woman finds her moral agency automatically impaired by the restrictions and limitations of domestic life.

Significantly, Melden is seduced by feminist argument because he does not take sufficient account of the details of the peculiar situations he is discussing. He recognizes that people are born helpless and dependent, but nowhere in his discussion of the domestic role of women does he consider the peculiar features of the relationship between mother and infant, even though he refers time and again to the obligations of *fathers* to their children. If our concept of a person did not refer to a being who is born helpless and is dependent in a special way on the care of its mother — an infant's father cannot, for obvious reasons, be accused of irresponsibility if *he* does not nurse his child — then, of course, feminist argument would be wholly in order. But given the fact of human life that Melden himself emphasizes (that we are all born helpless and dependent) the demand of women, particularly mothers, for the right to pursue their interests without qualification and uncontested ought to be regarded as abstract and groundless. Perhaps it is because Melden does not think seriously enough of men and women as *embodied* intelligences — and therefore of the crucial biological differences between the sexes that mean that the obligations of fathers and of mothers to their children are not totally symmetrical — that he ignores his own admonition that each situation must be judged according to its own merits; he happily applauds the fact that

many women have come to resent the position of subservience to which they have been relegated by the male-dominated society of which they are members and, with it, the idea that the right that women have to pursue their interests is the 'right' they have to assist, serve and cater to the more important endeavors that are reserved for men only. (p. 176)

In addition, he is probably drawn inevitably towards this judgement because he shares the rationalist prejudice that masculine activities depend on agency in a way that traditional, domestic, feminine activities do not. This is why he claims that the restriction of women to the domestic sphere is an instance of 'the violation of the right of a person as agent' (ibid., p. 174). But this conclusion is unwarranted, as we saw in the discussion of the issues surrounding the relation of women to reason in chapter 1.

Clearly, I am not denying that there may be certain ways of treating women which do reduce them to sex objects. Being a mother in our society may do just this because of the sterile surroundings in which the role of mothering often occurs and with the fact that the social context of child-bearing is itself sometimes a negative and rejecting one.[6] In any event, the important point for

---

[6] Cf., for example, Kitzinger, *Women as Mothers*, chapter 2, 'The Motherhood Trap'.

the moment is that to treat a woman as a person need not exclude, when relevant, an emphasis on her role as mother and wife. There is nothing demeaning and impairing about bringing children into the world and rearing them (unless certain prejudices are at work), and one can only wonder how our conception of a person *is* to be restored to its normal use in philosophical discourse if we talk of those who care for infants as being reduced automatically to sex objects. Perhaps it is no wonder that we consistently resist the need to restore our conception of a person to its normal use if we are afraid to admit that the idea of equal rights is, in the context of a discussion about family relations, an abstract concept, plausible only if one ignores the asymmetrical nature of the relation of mothers and fathers to their children.

Failure to recognize that our conventions have a basis in nature is, perhaps, the reason why the well-known paediatrician Dr Spock is also forced into an incoherent position. In an attempt to extricate himself from previous sexist tendencies, Spock aims to be egalitarian in the latest edition of his book *Baby and Child Care*.[7] He makes an effort, for example, to include men, and not only women, among his readers, and he advises that couples should assume they both 'have an equal *right* to a career with the least possible disruption' (p. 38), with care and responsibility for the infant falling equally on both of them. How precisely this is to be achieved, however, is difficult to see, as Spock also criticizes our society for the ways in which it puts distance between mothers and their babies. In many of the non-industrial parts of the world, he asserts, most babies are held against their mothers all day long by cloth carriers of one kind or another, share in all their mothers' movements as the women go about their regular jobs, are breast-fed the instant they whimper and hear and feel the vibrations of their mothers' words and songs. Our society, on the other hand, has invented, among other things,

anesthetized childbirth, so a mother misses the dramatic evidence of having created and borne a baby herself. . . . Babies are fed cow's milk

[7] See also his *Raising Children in a Difficult Time*.

from bottles so mothers and babies lose the opportunity for the most intimate bond in child-rearing. . . .

We've thought up the idea of propping bottles on babies' chests so that parents can be tending to other chores during the relatively short periods when young babies are awake and feeding. . . .

We put babies in pens where they can be kept out of trouble without having to be picked up, moved, or carried. (p. 6)

Yet Spock forgets that we are able to entertain the idea that a woman's career opportunities are not the same as a man's only as a result of *social* inequities, because ours is a society that does not care about the inevitable modifications that must be made to the mother—infant relationship — for example, bottle-feeding instead of breast-feeding, nursery care instead of a mother's individual love and attention, the deprecation of housework and its rejection in favour of work outside the home in offices, colleges, factories and so on — if women are to be able to compete on equal terms with men, and if men are to be expected to contribute their 'fair' share to the care of their infants. The restriction is thus based on nature and not on mere convention.

Spock is, of course, acutely aware of the fact that our society is one in which the abilities of women are both undervalued and underestimated. He hopes that the encouragement of achievement by women in the public sphere will change this. For example, he recommends that 'women in larger numbers could consider engineering, manufacturing, airline piloting, and the ministry.' However, a woman who has the intimate bond with her children that Spock so highly values will find herself in an intolerable situation as she tries to accommodate the needs of her children to a way of life that necessarily excludes children by the nature of its conditions and of the demands that such work makes on her. For instance, airline pilots on the more prestigious aeroplanes can be away from home for days at a time. This practical reality places a severe strain on human relationships. Perhaps it would be more to the point to question the desirability of such occupations for both men and women and the cost paid in terms of family and social life. Moreover, this still means that women would have to prove themselves by male norms in activities that are traditionally male and therefore lie outside the maternal role.

But if the crucial fact of womanhood (as feminists readily admit) is that women bear children and men do not, then surely a new sense of the worth of women should involve, above all, a revaluation of the maternal role. Instead it is forced into a secondary role both by 'liberated' women pursuing careers and by a society which tends to measure everything in terms of production goals. True, some feminists do think that housewifery is unjustifiably undervalued and seek to rectify this by demanding wages for mothers and housewives. This seems to me a retrograde and pernicious step, for the following reasons.

Marx criticized capitalism for reifying the relations between men by reducing them to a relationship based on a cash nexus, in which the 'worker sinks to the level of a commodity' (*Early Writings*, p. 322) and is no longer able to relate to others as real, living, particular individuals. The value of a man's life and his labour is reduced to the level of a thing: it is measured and quantified, disposed of and abused in the same way that commodities are. But men are not things, and therefore it is criminal to exploit them in this way. In fact, it is criminal to think of a man's life or any of his activities in terms of something on which a price can be fixed. As Simone Weil puts it in 'Human Personality':

Physical labour may be painful, but it is not degrading as such. . . .

To take a youth who has a vocation for this kind of work and employ him at a conveyor belt or as a piece-work machinist is no less a crime than to put out the eyes of the young Watteau and make him turn a grindstone. . . . it is sacrilege to degrade labour. . . .

If the workers felt this, if they felt that by being the victim they are in a certain sense the accomplice of sacrilege, their resistance would have a very different force from what is provided by the consideration of personal rights. It would not be an economic demand but an impulse from the depth of their being, fierce and desperate like that of a young girl who is being forced into a brothel; and at the same time it would be a cry of hope from the depth of their heart. . . .

Usually, when addressing them on their conditions, the selected topic is wages. . . .

In this way, they forget that the subject of the bargain, which they complain they are being forced to sell cheap and for less than the just price, is nothing other than their soul. (p. 17—18)

No price, no matter how high it may be, can justify the degradation and servitude of men in factories. In Marxian terms, Simone Weil is drawing attention to the fact that even in those movements that are struggling for the liberation of the workers, men's souls and lives are still thought of in terms of commodities, whereas the whole point is that 'we should reflect on the immorality implicit in the *evaluation* of a man in terms of *money*. . . .' (Marx, *Early Writings*, p. 263).

In the same way, the feminist suggestion that the love and care that a woman extends to her husband and children must have a price fixed on them if such a service is to command recognition and respect by society means that 'all the advances . . . within a false system turn out to be the greatest imaginable regression and at the same time they can be seen as perfidy taken to its logical conclusion' (ibid., p. 264). That is to say, when the care that one person bestows upon another is measured or evaluated in terms of *money*, it is automatically degraded and betrayed because love, by its very nature, is something that is given gratuitously. Moreover, the care that one person offers to another, and which exists in the social interaction between them as particular, living, flesh-and-blood human beings, becomes estranged and abstracted when its value shrinks and sinks into money: 'The existence of money in metal is only the official, visible expression of the money-soul which has percolated all the productions and movements of civil society.' (ibid., p. 262)

Feminists complain that housework and childcare are not recognized as work because women are not paid for them. Unfortunately, this complaint only confirms the values of a society which they purport to reject, for, according to Natalie Shainess, it shows that ours is a society of 'thing-oriented, impulse-ridden, narcissistically self-preoccupied people . . . increasingly dedicated to the acquisition of things' ('A Psychiatrist's View', p. 272). Nevertheless, it is true that society places little value on housework and childcare. Worse still, women themselves 'do not any longer know what to do with a home, how to use it, how to enjoy it, what to devote themselves to, as mothers' (ibid., p. 272).[8] Yet if the needs of infants and children and the needs of women as mothers are to be taken seriously, the home — i.e., family life — must retain a central place in any society. It is imperative that the importance of the woman's role in the home should be recognized. By emphasizing the right of women to have careers and by seeking the evaluation of the maternal role in terms of money, feminists have destroyed the possibility of constructive thought in this direction. So long as women do become mothers, an authentic feminism would have to begin with a serious discussion of these issues. As Natalie Shainess rightly remarks:

If there is a solution for women, it will come from a better set of values, education and society's help. It requires the recognition that nature has demanded much of them. To pursue interests beyond the home is an added burden, not an escape; and it demands great responsibility: it should be taken seriously by women, *and* society. It calls for an excellence upon which a high value should be placed, if there is concern about bettering the human condition. (ibid., p. 273)

We have to look for ways in which value can be placed upon

---

[8] This is inextricably bound up with the effects of an industrialized society, a fact which feminists sometimes recognize:

> The accomplishments of home production and the satisfaction of women's traditional sphere become intangible and fragmented. In the twentieth century the direct production in the family has been undermined, not just by poverty as it was in the nineteenth century, but also by plenty. New ways of processing, preserving and sealing food, new ways of storing food by refrigeration, mean that the nature of housework has become increasingly a service operation. The housewife maintains the male bread-winner and the children, not by producing goods herself, but by serving them with goods produced in the commodity system. . . . The old criteria by which women could feel their value have thus gone without new ones really taking root. (Rowbotham, *Woman's Consciousness, Man's World*, pp. 108—9)

femininity without resorting to money or 'masculine' activities as our frame of reference. This will be extremely difficult in an acquisitive society like ours, in which family life plays such a peripheral role in people's lives that even the question of having children has been degraded, reduced to the same level as the issue of whether or not to buy a new car, for instance.

But then this is all connected with the fact that the nuclear family of industrialized society is a degenerate form of family life, scarcely worthy of the name:

The family doesn't exist. What nowadays goes by that name is a minute collection of human beings grouped around each of us: father and mother, husband or wife, and children; brothers and sisters being already a little remote . . . . no one thinks nowadays about his ancestors who died fifty or even only twenty or ten years before his birth; nor about his descendants who will be born fifty or even only twenty or ten years after his death. (Weil, *The Need for Roots*, p. 95)

In fact, under modern conditions the view that the home and the family — the domains of woman — are sacrosanct is incoherent and hypocritical, for, as Marx scathingly pointed out:

The bourgeois claptrap about the family and education, about the hallowed co-relation of parent and child, becomes all the more disgusting, the more, by the action of modern industry, all family ties among the proletarians are torn asunder and their children transformed into simple articles of commerce and instruments of labour. ('Manifesto of the Communist Party', p. 66)

In other words, a society that really cared about family ties would condemn, absolutely and outright, anything that threatened them. (It would protect them against the assault by industry, for instance.) Unfortunately, however, it is now almost impossible for people to see what a serious loss the absence of a *genuine* family life is to society because of feminists' insistent declamation against the domestic role of women and because of the influence of Marxism, which has turned the whole discussion into an argument about the desirability or undesirability of privately owned property.[9] Tragically, there are deplorable consequences for human beings of a society in which there is neither a public nor a private realm, as Hannah Arendt points out:

Under modern circumstances, this deprivation of 'objective' relationships to others and of a reality guaranteed through them has become the mass phenomenon of loneliness, where it has assumed its most extreme and most antihuman form. [Arendt refers the reader to David Riesman's *The Lonely Crowd*.] The reason for this extremity is that mass society not only destroys the public realm but the private as well, deprives men not only of their place in the world but of their private home, where they once felt sheltered against the world and where, at any rate, even those excluded from the world could find a substitute in the warmth of the hearth and the limited reality of family life. (*The Human Condition*, pp. 58–9)

In any event, the destruction of the family (that is, the *extended* family), the institution in which a woman was actively supported by others in the care of her children and found company in her adult relatives who were close at hand, is undoubtedly one of the greatest contributory factors in the isolation and loneliness of the modern housewife.

The idea, then, that men should feel guilty about not taking a more active part in the day-to-day care of their *infants* and that women should indignantly feel resentment at being 'saddled' with the responsibility is, in Rousseau's opinion, a case of muddled thinking. What is at issue, he would have simply said, is that a man's life is not like that of a woman. Nevertheless, the feminist complaint that men do not sufficiently participate in the care of their *children* is a pertinent one. But this is related to the fact that even for men industrialization has removed all important work from the home to the factory or office. For with the best will in the world it is

[9] However, for an illuminating discussion of the very important relation between the existence of private property and the private realm, see Hannah Arendt's section 'The Private Realm: Property' in *The Human Condition*, pp. 58f.

almost impossible for a man who spends the greater part of each day
and of each week working away from home to be more than a remote
figure to his children, by contrast with their mother. The present
situation thus

contrasts with the system in a primitive or peasant society, where the
father works in and around the home, where activities he engages in
outside the home intermesh with the occupations he has inside it, and
where he takes his children with him to the fields and teaches them how
to do some of the simple tasks which are a part of the work he does.
(Kitzinger, *Women as Mothers*, p. 57)

Despite these obvious facts, feminists recommend not only that
fathers remain outside the home but also that women should join
them. Preposterously, it is suggested that this will improve relations
between parents and children.

So to say that biological facts matter and have consequences for the
nature of the relation between the sexes should not be seen as an
attempt to settle any questions: it only raises them. It does not mean
that there is not a multitude of different social arrangements which
could accommodate the fact that women have children. It does not
mean that women must be treated as if their sole purpose in life were
to bear children. On the other hand, it does mean that the problem
of how to reconcile the fact that women (and not men) have children
but also need and wish to be engaged in other purposeful, meaningful
activities and in relations with other adults is a real one. Feminists
rightly criticize our institutional structures for ignoring the latter
need but, conversely, their proposals fail to do justice to the other
horn of the dilemma, the issues thrown up by the human fact of
birth.

It is tempting to think that the failure of feminists to deal adequately
with the problem of birth and childhood in human life is an omission
that can easily be remedied. A fashionable response to the feminist
rejection of the maternal role is to point out that while the modern
idea that no mother should feel guilty about entrusting the care of

her infant to someone else as she pursues a career is a welcome and healthy one, there is nevertheless something special about the mother—infant relationship. A typical argument of this sort is advanced by Sheila Kitzinger, who advises:

Being a mother is an exciting occupation which demands all one's intelligence, all one's emotional resources and all one's capacity for speedy adjustment to new challenges. There is no reason why a woman should not want to have another career as well, but it is a pity that she should feel she ought to because she only is 'only a mother'. (ibid., p. 272)

Importantly, Kitzinger rightly notes that the maternal role has been unjustifiably deprecated in our society, but she misses the point of feminist argument in thinking that tomorrow's woman will be someone who is able to discover both the joys of domesticity and the excitement and status of having a career. She herself shows that this is a mere pipe-dream: if being a mother demands *all* a woman's attention, then following another career is a practical impossibility.

What in fact emerges from feminist argument, albeit tacitly, is that our conceptions of sex differences are not fundamentally *social* facts but, as Rousseau saw, are grounded in natural facts. Hence radical feminists stipulate that the liberation of women depends on their liberation not from sex *roles* but from being a woman — i.e., from the reproductive role. This argument is important because it reveals that essentially feminism is concerned only secondarily with the issues of rights and justice and that its real impetus seems to derive from a sort of rebellion against nature and not against patriarchal institutions.

What is actually behind the feminist insistence that men and women are equal? Generally, it is thought to be something like Plato's argument in the *Republic*.

Plato says that female watchdogs do just what male ones do, except that they are weaker and their lives are interrupted by birth. By analogy, he claims that the same is true of women: though they are weaker than men and their lives are interrupted by childbirth, they are otherwise the same and so should be given the same upbringing and tasks as men. It is then objected that this argument contradicts the principle on which the ideal state is constructed: that each person should do his own work, according to his nature. Therefore, since women differ in nature from men, they should have different functions in the city. But Plato dismisses this: certainly it is true that different natures should do different things, but it does not follow that men and women should do different things unless it can be shown that they have natures that are different in the important respect of affecting their capacity for the same pursuit; otherwise it would be like letting bald men, but not hairy men, be cobblers. In other words, the objector fails to show that there is any capacity peculiar to women. Hence, Plato concludes, there are no civic pursuits which belong to women as such or to men as such.

To an important extent, an argument such as Plato's inspires the traditional feminist demand for equality with men in all respects. Feminists have asserted that sex differences in themselves do not show that women are better suited to certain occupations than men; nor do they show that women should be treated differently from men. The fact that they are thought to matter in our society, as we have already seen, is related to the role that they play in maintaining a society based on male hegemony.

Yet it is significant — particularly if the feminist position is to be understood — that feminists have *not* been able to show that the difference between men and women is simply like that between male and female watchdogs, that in human life childbirth is akin to an isolated event like having a tooth out. Instead the thrust of feminist argument has made itself felt as the need to make a deliberate effort to bring the differences between male and female humans in line with that between male and female watchdogs; that is to say, to make the difference between the procreative role of men and women — like that of animals — much more like the difference between those who have had appendectomies (say) and those who have not. This is quite clearly evident, for example, in recent changes in attitudes towards maternity.

Traditionally, if economic or practical circumstances permitted, a woman gave up work, or continued to work only at home, on the birth of her children. Obviously, it was thought, she needed to be at home to nurse and care for them and to provide for their many different needs by cooking, sewing and so on. The father would make his contribution primarily in financial terms, while the mother's, at least while the children were very young, would be a physical and emotional one. It was assumed that she would naturally prefer to care for her baby and take full responsibility for it herself than go out to work and entrust it to the care of someone else. It was believed that for a woman to refuse this responsibility was to deprive herself of something infinitely precious: the special relationship that is born of the intimacy between a mother and her growing infant. For those women who did not regard this as the obvious choice, it was assumed (perhaps) that necessity rather than choice ruled the day.

According to feminists, however, this view was based on a falsehood perpetrated by men, for women do not want to remain at home looking after their babies and would prefer it if the responsibility for their infants could be entrusted to the care of state-run nurseries. The form their arguments take becomes clearer if we focus our attention on how modern legislation accommodates itself to the demand of women to retain a place for themselves in the public sphere despite pregnancy.

Working women who become pregnant are protected by various pieces of legislation: they may not be dismissed; their job is guaranteed if they return to work within a certain period of time, with the advantage of financial remuneration; and so on. The aim of legislation seems to be to create a sense of continuity in the transition between being a worker and being a mother. Consequently, the concept of maternity leave, for example, is very much akin to the notion of the sabbatical leave that a man might take from his work or of a prolonged holiday. To return to work is to get back to 'normal'; child-bearing is seen as an interruption in the woman's life, and on the part of the woman 'Children are viewed as a temporary constriction preventing desired experiences' (Kitzinger, *Women as Mothers*, p. 35). Hence there is little hint that maternity leave might rather be a period of adjustment to an event of enormous significance, capable of radically changing a person's life. There is little suggestion that initiation into motherhood means that the world will never be the same again; for, as in the case of bereavement, when the world changes because of the loss of someone close and dear, with birth the world changes because there is now another human being to love and care for and to whom a woman's life is bound. The fact that fresh and pressing demands will be made of the woman by the needs of the new arrival is carefully ignored, even though these demands are far from met by the time the infant is seven months, the age at which women are obliged to return to work. Indeed, as Kitzinger rightly remarks:

There is so little social recognition of what is actually involved in the fatiguing task of being a mother that women are usually made to explain their post-partum experience entirely in terms of internal states, their hormones, their psyches and their own inadequate personalities, instead of the realities of the situation as they adjust to the new occupational and emotional tasks of motherhood. . . . (p. 37)

The feminist insistence that it is unjust to curtail the career opportunities of women simply because they have children has, of course, done little to change this lack of recognition. Rather, the consequence of 'enlightened' legislation and the change in public opinion has been that a woman is regarded and treated as if she were childless, as if the event of birth were isolated and final, precisely so that she may continue to compete on 'equal' terms with her male colleagues. The fact that there is an infant, a human being, who is still really not much more than an appendage to her in terms of its physical and emotional needs, and will be so for some time yet, is either a source of embarrassment or — and understandably, from the point of view of an employer — a cause for annoyance.

Clearly, the legislation protecting the rights of the working mother presupposes that such changes are taken into account. However, it acknowledges them as a handicap, for which compensation is justly to be expected, rather than attempting to come to terms with the very specific problems of working women with infants and young children. How else can one regard the right of exhausted mothers to work as a victory for feminists? Yet the argument that the situation of women with children might justify discrimination against their working outside the home (say) or at certain hours is ruled out by feminists as unjust because, given the abstract terms in which their discussion is couched, they fear, for example, that 'Protective legislation against night work presents a difficult problem because it is grounds for discrimination against women within capitalism' (Rowbotham, *Women's Consciousness, Man's World*, p. 92). Rowbotham expresses this reservation even though she readily sees that the extension of such a right to women could make life intolerable for them:

Lyn Stevens works on the 10 p.m. to 6 a.m. shift at a light engineering factory in the East Midlands. She has two children, Elaine aged 8 and Mark aged 5. . . . She felt one of the worst aspects of night work for women is that whereas men on night work can often come home in the morning and go straight to bed, women started to do a 'bit of tidying or washing' and then found they only had time for a few hours sleep.
    'I get so tired,' she said, 'and it's hard not to take it out on the children. I catch up at weekends. My husband helps me a lot. I think it's a disgrace for anybody to have to work nights. It destroys your life.'
(Valerie Clark, 'When Did You Last See Your Wife?', *Socialist Worker* 10 October 1970, cited by Rowbotham, p. 93)

This sort of case shows unequivocally that there is something corrupt both in a society which tolerates such situations and in feminist arguments which propose that the refusal to grant work to mothers — no matter what such work may entail — is necessarily an injustice. I am not saying that we should therefore ignore the awful problems of mothers who are in financial straits; rather, the point is that it might be wiser to look in an altogether different direction — in a direction, perhaps, in which the fundamental issues hardly revolve around sexism and feminism — than that traditionally insisted upon by feminist rhetoric if a genuine and humane solution to such problems is to be found.

Equally, the case cited above shows that there is something inadequate about the ideal implicit in protective legislation, that justice consists in treating a mother equally and the same as everyone else. The possibility of respecting the special needs of working mothers is threatened if the role of a woman *qua* mother is made incidental to, rather than central to, her circumstances and her plea for justice. Thus if an employer were to suggest to a pregnant employee that she consider giving up work on the birth of her child, he would not necessarily have to be regarded as a sexist. Similarly, it is no longer obviously valid to argue that the idea that a mother has to face peculiar problems because of her situation *qua* mother is an invention of the patriarchal mind.

The upshot of all this is that the biological differences between men and women are significant ones. Clearly, it is not just because of social conditioning that men do not need maternity leave. It is because they neither become pregnant, nor give birth, nor suckle their offspring. And the notion of *compensatory* rights, which is the stuff of legislation on women's rights, explicitly reveals that feminists are quite sure that the undisputed biological differences between the sexes matter enough to interfere in the lives of women, even at the irreducible, biological level, in a way that they do not in the lives of men.

In short, the legislation for equal rights tends to aim specifically to provide cultural compensation for the fact that women are supposedly unfairly restricted by their reproductive role. Essentially, the demand for nurseries, for example — when it is not thought of as a means of enabling women to escape from the isolation and loneliness to which they and their children are often condemned by the nature of the society in which we live[10] — is a demand that women be provided

[10] Cf., for example, the following remarks by Linda Gordon:

Families free men to work by harnessing women to raise children. . . . This is destructive. It keeps women and children isolated, deprives children of the company of men most of the time, and deprives women of the company of adults, which is enough to turn an adult brain into mush — if you're not a mother and don't believe it, try spending 48 hours with children only. ('Functions of the Family', p. 182)

with some means of liberating themselves from the inevitable restrictions of having children. This sort of demand is not a call to men to do their 'fair' share. For, indeed, what 'fair' contribution can a man make to the procreative role? He cannot become pregnant. He cannot suffer birth pangs. He cannot suckle his baby. Crucially, the fact that there is something very incoherent in the claim that men must do their 'fair' share has led certain feminists to argue that some altogether more radical solution is required.

6

Nature and Convention II: Feminism and the Oppression of Women

What is required for women's liberation is put in uncompromising terms by Shulamith Firestone, in an attempt to show what a feminist revolution would have to look like. Central to her position in *The Dialectic of Sex* is the argument that the child-bearing role of women is not as incidental to a woman's life as an argument like Plato's would seem to imply and as liberal feminists would like to think. Consequently, according to her account — in striking contrast to what would appear to be the orthodox feminist position — the *biological* facts of womanhood form the axis around which the whole feminist debate must ultimately revolve.

She would agree with Rousseau that the differences between the sexes are not of the same order as those between hairy men and bald men. This is because, in pregnancy, women are unable to pursue their interests as singlemindedly as before because of the discomfort they experience. With the birth of children, they are confined to the home, to giving children the care that they need. And thus confined to the home, they inevitably lack the power and control over their lives that are necessary if they are to resist economic dependence on men and the supposedly inevitable oppression that goes with it. Says Firestone: 'The immediate assumption of the layman that the unequal division of the sexes is "natural" may be well-founded. . . . Unlike economic class, sex class sprang directly from a biological reality: men and women were created different, and not equal.' (p.'16)

Radical feminists emphasize, then, that the mere fact — that is,

115

the biological fact — of being a woman is an oppressive one. The tyrant is not man at all but nature: men simply take advantage of the situation, which is already weighted in their favour: 'The heart of woman's oppression is her child-bearing and child-rearing role.' (p. 73) Hence the possibility of artificial reproduction and the free availability of birth control, in the form of both contraceptives and abortion, represent finally the true means to realize the liberation of women. Women have to be liberated, first and foremost, from the shackles of their biology. This is why Firestone asserts that 'feminism is the inevitable response to the development of a technology capable of freeing women from the tyranny of their sexual-reproductive roles' (p. 37). Of course, enormous resistance to such technologizing of procreation can be expected, but only because the oppression of women by nature is fundamental to patriarchy and instrumental in helping men to uphold it. Nevertheless, the radical feminist urges, if women truly wish for liberation, truly wish for equality, they must be prepared to fight for this opportunity to eradicate *all* differences between the sexes. In short, only when the biological differences between the sexes are obliterated will it be possible to speak of the sexes as genuinely equal.

Firestone's contention is that the liberation of women depends, then, on the elimination of a fundamental fact of nature: the undisputed differences between the sexes. Thus she makes explicit something that is hardly realized by most feminists, namely, that if a person's sex is incidental to personhood and men and women are (or should be) equal, women will be better off only when biological differences, causing the inconveniences that they do, are eliminated. Further, she models her argument on a Marxian, materialist one in an attempt to show that there cannot be changes in the super-structure of patriarchy — its political ideology, social inequities and so on — without changes in its base: hence the need for technological changes in the methods of reproduction. Interestingly, Firestone violently rejects the usual feminist arguments that women's oppression derives from patriarchal culture, and this is precisely because she is acutely aware of the fact that our conceptions of sex differences are conventions very much rooted in natural facts and rejects outright the notion that women were not oppressed in matriarchal societies. On the contrary, women have always been oppressed because 'it was woman's reproductive biology that accounted for her original and continued oppression, and not some sudden patriarchal revolution, the origins of which Freud himself was at a loss to explain' (p. 74). According to Firestone's account, the argument based on convention does not adequately explain the oppression of women. Against Kitzinger, she would argue that the idea that there can be anything fulfilling in being a mother is a contradiction in terms. To be a mother is *ipso facto* to be oppressed. Indeed, while women continue to give birth, they will never experience any authentic liberation.

Firestone is, in fact, following Simone de Beauvoir here and developing a thought that is central to Beauvoir's account of the relation of woman to her biology. Claiming that woman is subordinate to biology, she construes the peculiar features of the female anatomy in terms of a struggle between biology and woman in which biology is all too often the victor:

in woman's subordination to the species . . . we find the most striking conclusion of this survey: namely, that woman is of all mammalian females . . . the one who is most profoundly alienated (her individuality the prey of outside forces) . . . [and] in no other is enslavement of the organism to reproduction more imperious. . . . Crises of puberty and the menopause, monthly 'curse', long and often difficult pregnancy, painful and sometimes dangerous childbirth . . . these are characteristic of the human female. . . . In comparison with her the male seems infinitely favoured: his sexual life is not in opposition to his existence as a person, and biologically it runs an even course, without crises and generally without mishap. (*The Second Sex*, p. 59)

The idea of biology as a mighty tyrant against whom woman is continually struggling recurs with persistence throughout Beauvoir's book; every physical phenomenon she discusses is seen to vindicate the thesis of her basic schema. Thus she asserts that a woman's perception of the fact that she is pregnant confronts her with the brutal conditions of her enslavement:

she knows that her body is destined to transcend itself; day after day a growth arising from her flesh but foreign to it is going to enlarge within her; she is the prey of the species, which imposes its mysterious laws upon her, and as a rule this subjection to strange outer forces frightens her, her fright being manifested in morning sickness and nausea. These are in part brought on by the modification of the gastric secretions produced at this time; but if this reaction, unknown in other mammals, is an important one in woman, the cause of it is psychic; it expresses the sharpness that at this time marks the conflict, in the human female, between the species and the individual. (p. 479)

Beauvoir is not saying that in certain cultures it is impossible for women to think of pregnancy in any other way, but she is stipulating that the biological facts of the situation force women to think of pregnancy in just this way. In other words, it would seem that woman's struggle is against nature and not against convention if her true individuality is to be manifested in being liberated from the bonds of biology. And in so far as Rousseau is justified in arguing that inequality between the sexes is based not on prejudice but on nature (see above, p. 87), the radical feminist argument typified by those of Beauvoir and Firestone seems to touch the nerve of the problem in the whole discussion concerning equal rights. *This* is what women have to challenge if the demand for equal rights is to make any sense at all — hence my reasons for stating earlier that the women's liberation movement is a rebellion against nature.

Indeed, crucial to radical feminist argument is the assertion that it is precisely because the relative impotence of women in the public sphere can be justified on the grounds of the restrictions imposed upon them by biological constraints that the real oppressor of women is nature. The root of the oppression lies in the so-called original division of labour between the sexes for the purposes of procreation. Consequently, the demand for birth control, abortion and artificial reproduction is absolutely fundamental to any coherent programme for the liberation of women. This is why traditional discussions about the status of the foetus in disputes over abortion have little, if any, relevance to the real issues at hand. For abortion, like artificial reproduction, is the chief weapon against the aggressor and offers the only authentic means of liberation from oppression (and, at the same time, from being a woman), as Lucinda Cisler points out in 'Unfinished Business':

Because women have wombs and bear children . . . different reproductive roles are *the* basic dichotomy in humankind, and have been used to rationalize all the other ascribed differences between men and women and to justify all the oppression women have suffered.

Without the full capacity to limit her own reproduction, a woman's other 'freedoms' are tantalizing mockeries that cannot be exercised. With it, the others cannot long be denied, since the chief rationale for denial disappears. (pp. 274–5)

From this point of view, then, to suggest that woman should be educated to try to come to terms with the biological conditions of her life and to accept them, as Rousseau proposes, would be to suggest that she ought to accept her oppression. It would be like telling a black slave to accept that his enslavement is based on the incontrovertible fact that white rule is supreme and invincible. However, this only follows — the analogy only works and feminism itself, as a system of thought, ultimately only makes sense — if it can be shown to be intelligible to speak of biology as an oppressor.

The assertion that women's liberation must be grounded in the abolition of the 'original division of labour' is an idea that is parasitic on Marxian economic theory. This is natural because radical feminism grew from a spare rib of leftist revolutionary politics. It is connected with Engels' arguable idea that the differences in the procreative role of the sexes can be construed as a division of labour.

Strictly speaking, the term 'division of labour' is used to describe the division of one task, easily undertaken by one person, into a series of minute operations shared among a number of people. Generally, the reasons for such division is that it facilitates greater efficiency and economy of production, a consequence of which is the segregation of people into different groups, arbitrarily determined by the section of the operation in which they happen to be engaged.

This mode of production inevitably throws up a mountain of problems which need not concern us here except to note that the aim of abolishing the division of labour in this context — to reinstate the relation between a person and his work as an integrated whole — is in practice realizable. In fact, the desirability of such a goal depends for its force on the fact that a mode of production based on the division of labour is not necessary and inevitable but is relative only to certain sorts of economic goal.

Now, in order to make sense of the notion of a division of labour between the sexes, it is necessary to think of a single subject in which such division is not present. Feminists do this by presuming as the single subject mankind or society, which has divided its labours among men and women. But this is a plausible move only if one accepts the 'communistic fiction', which as Gunnar Myrdal points out in *The Political Element in the Development of Economic Theory*, 'amounts to the assertion that society must be conceived as a single subject' (p. 154). Can this be done? Myrdal rightly insists: 'This, however, is precisely what cannot be conceived. If we tried, we would be attempting to abstract from the essential fact that social activity is the result of the intentions of several individuals.' (p. 154) Thus while the term 'division of labour' is appropriate to describe modern labour conditions in which one activity is atomized into innumerable minute manipulations, it cannot apply either to the so-called division of labour in professional specialization[1] or to the different procreative role of the sexes. Following Myrdal, Hannah Arendt observes that division of labour in professional specialization

can be so classified only under the assumption that society must be conceived as one single subject, the fulfilment of whose needs are then subdivided by 'an invisible hand' among its members. The same holds true, *mutatis mutandis*, for the odd notion of a division of labor between the sexes. It presumes as its single subject man-kind, the human species, which has divided its labor among men and women. (*The Human Condition*, pp. 47—8)

---

[1] This is connected with my remarks on androgyny in chapter 3.

That this is precisely what is presumed by feminists emerges explicitly and persistently from Simone de Beauvoir's account of the female anatomy as a struggle between the individual and the species. Importantly, this presumption raises questions about how far the notion of oppression can play an intelligible role in any discussion of a woman's procreative role. The kinds of use that commonly give the term 'oppression' its sense occur in situations in which power or force is cruelly and despotically exerted by someone or by a group of people over others: 'Now therefore, behold, the cry of the children of Israel is come unto me: and I have also seen the oppression wherewith the Egyptians oppress them.' (*Exodus* 3: 9); 'The children of Israel and the children of Judah were oppressed together: and all that took them captive held them fast; they refused to let them go.' (*Jeremiah* 1: 33) Hence to talk of oppression intelligibly we need two forces: one enslaving and the other enslaved. We need human subjects who are involved in a drama in which one group of agents is enslaved or rendered passive by another. In other words, the notions of agency and action must be applicable to both parties if the notion of oppression is to be appropriate. Consequently, however cruelly someone might treat his animals, we would never describe the animals as oppressed. A slave, on the other hand, is considered oppressed precisely because, as a human agent, he is reduced to a passive object:

The 'slave by nature' then is he that can and therefore does belong to another, and he that participates in the reasoning faculty so far as to understand but not so as to possess it. For the other animals serve their owner not by exercise of reason but passively. The use, too, of slaves hardly differs at all from that of domestic animals; from both we derive that which is essential for our bodily needs. (Aristotle, *Politics*, p. 34)

In effect, in admitting that slaves differ from animals, even if it is only because they merely share the reasoning faculty, Aristotle provides enough evidence for us to see that the alleged parallel between slaves and domestic animals is a spurious one; that is, he says enough for the issue of the oppression of slaves to be raised intelligibly.

Given that these are the sorts of conditions in which utterances about oppression may be made, it is difficult to see how it can be argued that a woman's biology oppresses her. Beauvoir, for instance, talks of woman as being 'in the iron grasp of the species' (*The Second Sex*, p. 58) and argues that her body 'is something other than herself', that 'her individuality is the prey of outside forces' (p. 57). Yet unless one is prepared at least to assume some kind of Cartesian dualism here, it is hard to see why there should be, and how there can be, this supposed conflict or opposition between body and mind, between biology and the individual. Such an assertion is all the more curious when Beauvoir herself claims to be following Merleau-Ponty and Sartre — two philosophers both strenuously opposed to any form of Cartesian dualism — by stating that 'woman, like man, *is* her body' (ibid.). Sartre goes to some length to show that in so far as the body is a 'necessary characteristic of the for-itself', it is not 'the product of an arbitrary decision on the part of a demiurge', nor is the union of soul and body 'the contingent bringing together of two substances radically distinct' (*Being and Nothingness*, pp. 408–9).

But Beauvoir opposes Sartre in assuming just what he is concerned to discredit. For even if a dualism between body and mind could be accepted without reservation, there is a further difficulty with the view proposed by her. This is the idea that the individuality or person of woman is oppressed and made passive by something we should not normally be tempted to think of as being autonomous or active: mere given, natural, biological facts. Beauvoir makes it look as though woman were struggling with an active force by making precisely what Hannah Arendt observed to be an unfounded assumption in feminist argument: she invents a fictional 'subject', the human species — in Sartre's terms, a 'demiurge' — to give her argument the plausibility it so desperately needs. And without this fiction, the argument has, of course, to fall flat. Other feminists, like Firestone, do not use this fiction, but only because they fail to see that without it their arguments have no starting-point.

It is as if we should imagine a man prosecuting a natural object, like a tree, for falling on his son and killing him. That is to say, there are important distinctions to be made between conditions made by men or agents and those which have natural causes: the many people who suffer and die in an earthquake are the victims of a natural disaster and not of a manmade one. If someone were to react to the earthquake with the same range of responses that might naturally be felt at an atomic explosion, we would consider him mad. In the event of an earthquake, there is no one we can blame, no one we can punish, no one from whom we may seek retribution. Conversely, in the event of an atomic explosion, we would regard it as odd if someone were to say, with assumed profundity, something like 'What must be must be' or remark that in situations of this sort men can only bow down with humility and patience, as did Job in the face of his afflictions, before those forces that are so much greater than themselves. A moral condemnation, so appropriate in the second case, would be foolish in the first because only human agents can commit deeds which are good or bad.

Accordingly, there is nothing out of place in feminist insistence that women ought actively to resist and condemn their oppression by certain groups of people in certain sorts of situation. However, to say as feminists do that women are oppressed by their biological condition is to misuse the grammar of the word oppression and is to say something that is unintelligible and, in many ways, disturbing.

A common feminist argument is to claim that sexual inequality is analogous to racial inequality. This may be true, but it is important to see just what has to be acknowledged for the analogy to be a genuine one. We have just seen that, given the reality of the constraints that biological facts impose upon the lives of women, feminists are inclined to argue that women are oppressed not by patriarchy or sexist conventions but by nature. Hence the real problem with being a woman is not that one lives in a society that is unjust and discriminates against women, but that one *is* a woman in a world that is obviously and necessarily — so the argument goes — more acceptable, desirable and human if one is a man: that is, a female human being minus the procreative role. This, we saw, is why Firestone contends that woman's child-bearing role is at the heart of her oppression.

What would a black person have to say about his or her situation for the analogy to hold? I suggest that an argument such as the following would have to be insisted upon. Assuming that all had been said and done to bring about racial equality, a black person would have to complain that the real difficulty with being black was not that he lived under a system of apartheid but that his skin was black instead of white. A black woman could claim that white women had an unfair advantage — albeit one based on nature — in having such features as rosy complexions and straight hair: for a black woman genuine liberation would have to consist in the free availability of skin-lightening creams and hair-straightening compounds or the use of wigs.

Would a feminist really think it unjust if white biologists refused to expend vast sums of money on research into how the colour of a person's skin might be controlled and changed? Would a feminist really think that the companies selling skin-lightening creams to black people would be rendering them a service in offering them the long-awaited technological key to their liberation? Clearly not. Yet whereas an important feature of black consciousness has been the realization that the natural facts of being black and being ethnically different from whites are not inherently oppressive, but become so only in the subhuman conditions to which black people in racist countries are condemned, for feminists an analogous view of their situation is ruled out *a priori*, for reasons which are central and integral to their position.

Feminists might still argue that although it does not make sense to talk of biology as an *oppressive* fact in the lives of women, nevertheless biology does constrain them. And they could be freed from such constraint. Why should women not choose to come to terms with biological constraints by controlling them and manipulating them, thereby gaining a measure of freedom? As Rudolph Schaffer puts it:

There is . . . no reason why the mothering role should not be filled as competently by males as by females. . . . technological progress, in this respect as in so many others, can free mankind from biological constraints and make possible new patterns of social living. Technology has perfected milk formulas and the feeding bottle so that anyone, of either sex, can satisfy a baby's hunger. That same technology has provided us with so many mechanical aids that sheer physical strength is now rarely needed: women can just as well press the button that starts an agricultural harvester or fires a nuclear rocket. And, finally, biologists give us reason to think that even the process of birth, in its natural form, is not sacrosanct — that it may eventually be possible to grow a foetus not in a womb but in an artificial environment from which it is delivered in due course. Thus all the original reasons for confining child care to women are disappearing: *mother need not be a woman!* (*Mothering*, pp. 111–12)

In Schaffer's exhortation to liberate women from mothering is crystallized a certain view of the relation between freedom and power; freedom is thought of specifically in terms of the degree of technological control that a person has over natural facts. According to this view, the adoption of any course of action is justified if it can be shown simply to increase a person's freedom in terms of such control. Essentially, this is behind the feminist insistence that any technological control over reproduction must be a good thing. The reason for assuming that the notion of freedom is linked with technological control in just this way becomes clear in the light of a certain conception of agency and action and of how the distinction between human beings and beasts shows itself in certain features of man's, as opposed to woman's, relation to nature.

We noted above that rationalists tend to think that only those activities for which there is no parallel in the animal world are distinctly human. An important corollary to this conception is the view that human reason or human agency — notably the fact that man is an active creature, while animals are passive — displays man's superiority over beasts through the control and power he has over nature and over his life. Man distinguishes himself from beasts by not having to remain in perpetual subservience to the forces of nature and by transforming nature to satisfy his needs. This is why Hegel, as we saw, says that while the prominent point of the curse is that man must work by the sweat of his brow, work nevertheless constitutes a victory of man over nature: 'The beasts have nothing more to do but to pick up the materials required to satisfy their wants: man on the contrary can only satisfy his wants by transforming, and as it were originating the necessary means.' (see p. 5 above) The power of human reason is demonstrated by the manipulatory power that man has over his life, in contradistinction to the impotence that animals are condemned to endure. It clearly follows, it is argued, that man distinguishes himself more and more clearly from animals as he gains greater control over his environment and over his life. And since what distinguishes men from animals is, in essence, the faculty of reason, greater control over the natural conditions of life displays the growth of reason and freedom. Moreover, since the assumed equation between animality, degeneracy and savagery is taken as axiomatic in such discussions, it appears incontrovertible that the more dramatically the distinction between man and beasts shows itself in the degree of such control, the further human life is removed from degeneracy and savagery and the closer it is to a life based on knowledge and freedom.

Feminists are impressed with the rationalist account given of the relation between agency and man's dominion over nature but add forcefully that the real dominion of nature must include the dominion by women over *their* natural functions, namely, the reproductive organs. This is why they angrily retort that it is unfair of men to restrict or license research into, and the use of, methods for controlling reproduction.

Feminist thinking finds its most lucid expression in Beauvoir's *The Second Sex*. Beauvoir generously acknowledges that men have indeed given their existence value and worth, and have distinguished it from mere animal life, by conquering nature and by triumphing over natural forces. She happily endorses the view that men are infinitely more human than women precisely because they have transcended nature:

In the animal, the freedom and variety of male activities are vain because no project is involved. . . . Whereas in serving the species, the human male also remodels the face of the earth, he creates new instruments, he invents, he shapes the future. . . . *The support of life became for man an activity and a project through the invention of the tool*; but in maternity woman remained closely bound to her body, like an animal. . . . Man's design is not to repeat himself in time: it is to take control of the instant and mould the future. It is male activity that in creating values has made of existence itself a value; this activity has prevailed over the confused forces of life; it has subdued Nature and Woman. (pp. 89—91; my italics)

Beauvoir therefore concedes that, to a large extent, women have not yet defined themselves as distinct from animals because bondage to the biological facts of pregnancy, birth and suckling cannot give women meaning, nor do these truly distinguish women from animals because such facts are not 'activities':

they are natural functions; no project is involved; and that is why woman found in them no reason for a lofty affirmation of her existence — she submitted passively to her biologic fate. The domestic labours that fell to her lot because they were reconcilable with the cares of maternity imprisoned her in repetition and immanence; they were repeated from day to day in an identical form, which was perpetuated almost without change from century to century; they produced nothing new. (p. 88)

Consequently, because the notion of the transcendence of nature is made central to the conception of man's distinctness from animals, it becomes imperative, feminists argue, to see that women can become authentic agents only by transcending, so to speak, their reproductive functions. Men display their prowess and their capacity for action through their manipulatory power over the world. By contrast, women display their impotence, their passivity and their incapacity for action as free human beings precisely to the extent that they do not have any choice *vis-à-vis* their reproductive functions.

 Here again we have a clue to why the right to control their bodies through contraception and abortion is such a crucial demand for feminists. It might be said that contraception and abortion are to women what the tool was to man. Through birth control women are supposedly able, finally, to control and intervene in a natural process and *ipso facto* to discover their agency as creative, active, free beings. In a sense, it is precisely because the Roman Catholic Church, for instance, forbids the use of contraceptives, on the grounds that these interfere with a *natural* process, that feminists are bound to assert that the Church is motivated by a desire to condemn women to passivity.

Similarly, the feminist demand that women have the right to abortion is essentially the argument that women have a right to be agents, to be active, to distinguish themselves from animals. Admittedly, the argument for abortion takes the form that since it is the woman considering an abortion who has to face the consequences of an undesired or inconvenient pregnancy, *she* should have the liberty to decide whether or not to terminate the pregnancy. That feminists tend to be unmoved totally by the argument of the pro-life lobby — namely, that abortion need be neither the most obvious nor the only 'solution', particularly if concrete, active support is given by the community to pregnant women in difficult circumstances and to single women with children — clearly suggests that they do not consider abortion as, first and foremost, a desperate response to a difficult problem.

In fact, Simone de Beauvoir sanctions abortion for the very reasons I give. She asserts that through abortion and contraception female human society rises above animal life and shows that it is 'never abandoned wholly to nature. And for about a century the reproductive function in particular has no longer been at the mercy solely of biological chance; it has come under the voluntary control of human beings' (p. 467). This is why she sees no difficulty in maintaining that legislation in favour of abortion represents an enormous advance for women because the use of it apparently represents the exercise of freedom and agency. The strength of the refusal to permit abortion, she therefore says, can be used as a gauge to measure how reluctant men are to grant women freedom: 'How lively anti-feminism still is can be judged by the eagerness of certain men to reject everything favourable to the emancipation of women.' (p. 469) Yet, at the same time, she herself describes abortion as one of the cruellest experiences a woman is ever likely to have to undergo, with the further unjustified implication that it is forced upon woman by man:

Men universally forbid abortion, but individually they accept it as a convenient solution of a problem; they are able to contradict themselves with careless cynicism. But woman feels these contradictions in her wounded flesh; she is as a rule too timid for open revolt aganist masculine bad faith; she regards herself as the victim of an injustice that makes her a criminal against her will, and at the same time she feels soiled and humiliated. She embodies in concrete and immediate form, in herself, man's fault; he commits the fault, but he gets rid of it by putting it off on her; he merely says some words in a suppliant, threatening, sensible, or furious tone: he soon forgets them; it is for her to interpret these words in pain and blood. Sometimes he says nothing, he just fades away. . . .

[Women then] learn to believe no longer in what men say. . . . the one thing they are sure of this is this rifled and bleeding womb, these shreds of crimson life, this child that is not there. . . . For many women the world will never be the same. (p. 474)

The general horror people have of abortion, then, is not as irrational as Beauvoir suggests at first. It seems she is forced into this contradictory position because she hangs her whole discussion of the humanity of woman on the degree of control woman has over her reproductive functions. And so Rousseau's contention, for instance, that women should accept their constraints, and that society should be structured in such a way that it helps rather than hinders them in doing this, would, according to Beauvoir's account, be tantamount to the assertion that mankind should never have striven to rise beyond the animal kingdom. This follows, however, only if one accepts the rationalist conception of action.

The notion of action is indeed important in the distinction between human beings and beasts because it can be argued that what distinguishes us from animals is the aspect of agency. But what Beauvoir does is to telescope the notion of agency to include only power and control over natural facts. That is to say, she thinks of action essentially in terms of the practical changes in the world which an agent is able to bring about. This is hardly surprising, for such action is certainly one very striking way in which humans reveal that they are distinct from animals. It includes a range of achievement, from artistic creation to scientific discovery. However, she fails to see — and she is certainly not alone in this failure — that the notion of control or manipulatory power over events is not crucial to, and certainly not synonymous with, the notion of agency.

One obvious difference is that the manipulatory power that an agent is able to exercise over certain events or over certain natural facts may be absolutely restricted by an injunction of a moral or a legal nature without in any way impairing his agency. Indeed, agency would have to be presupposed to make the notion of a moral or legal sanction intelligible. This might be another way of clarifying what was wrong with Melden's view that the agency of women is impaired by the moral injunction imposed upon them to play a special role in caring for their children. That is, Melden conflates the notion of agency with 'masculine', productive action and forgets that caring for children, though it may be considered unimportant in our society, is nevertheless something only an agent can do.

If anything, what makes certain behaviour constitute the action of an agent is something that is crucially dependent neither on the degree of control his actions have over nature, nor on the fact that a particular action bears absolutely no resemblance to anything that an animal has ever done, but on the fact that it is committed against a background of thoughts and intentions. Here again we see that even where there are similarities between animal and human behaviour, they are nearly always superficial ones. Hence someone may still be an agent and capable of action even if his or her life is characterized by powerlessness to effect productive changes or to gain control over events. An outstanding example of this is afforded by the patience with which a person can suffer affliction (cf. *The*

Book of Job). Here is how Kierkegaard, for example, characterizes it:

Is patience not precisely that courage which voluntarily accepts unavoidable suffering? . . . Thus, patience, if one may put it in this way, performs an even greater miracle than courage. Courage voluntarily chooses suffering that may be avoided; but patience achieves freedom in unavoidable suffering. By his courage, the free one voluntarily lets himself be caught, but by his patience the prisoner effects his freedom — although not in the sense that need make the jailer anxious or fearful. . . . One can be forced into the narrow prison, one can be forced into lifelong sufferings, and necessity is the tyrant; but one cannot be forced into patience. . . . When the victim of unavoidable suffering bears it patiently, one says of him, 'to his shame, he is coerced, and he is making a virtue out of necessity'. Undeniably he is making a virtue out of a necessity, that is just the secret, that is certainly a most accurate designation for what he does. . . . He brings a determination of freedom out of that which is determined as a necessity. (*Purity of Heart*, pp. 152—3)

An important corollary to the fact that agency need not involve control over events is that for something to count as knowledge, it need not necessarily include anything that might look like dominion over nature.[2] To many people this is the only way of seeing it, because they have tended to think of action only as that which is productive of changes and have forgotten that, as Georg von Wright rightly observes:

Action has a 'passive' counterpart which is usually called forbearance. Forbearance can be distinguished from mere passivity, not acting, by being intentional passivity. By forbearing one does not strictly produce things or prevent things from happening, but by forbearing one can let things change or leave them unchanged. These changes and not changes are the outer aspect of forbearance. . . . The immediate outer aspect of forbearance is, normally, a state of muscular rest or, exceptionally,

[2] Think, for example, of the Trukese methods of navigation (see pp. 45f).

muscular activity which one 'lets go on' although one could restrain the movements. (*Explanation and Understanding*, pp. 90—1)

With this in mind, the difficulty of recognizing anything in the procreative functions of women that can reasonably be described as the free act of an agent comes from presuming that all action has to stand against the thoughts and intentions appropriate to productive or manipulative action. For, judged from that vantage point, intentional passivity must seem ineffectual and inferior.

Simone de Beauvoir says, we noted above, that birth and suckling are not activities because they are natural. The implication of her argument seems to be that they become activities when they are no longer merely natural but are transformed in some way by human hands, perhaps by anaesthetizing birth or by bottle-feeding. This is connected with her contention that agency consists in having control over nature because such control is absent in the life of animals. She fails to see, however, that even a man who produces something is an agent only because his behaviour is set in a wider context of aims and cognitions. This is why no matter how well elephants at a circus may 'dance', they can only be said to be performing tricks and not actions. Similarly, the robots who now 'make' cars in a production line, no matter how impressive the operations they carry out, will never be agents.[3] Thus the notion of agency that is really at stake here is related not to the question of whether the suffering of a woman in childbirth can be brought under our technical control but to the issue of whether it can be subsumed under the aspect of intentionality.

Imagine two women suffering labour. One is thoroughly overcome by the brutality of the pangs she has to bear. She feels herself a victim of the raging pains tearing her insides and feels herself passive, 'a suffering and tortured instrument' (Beauvoir, *The Second Sex*, p. 486) The possibility of anaesthetizing the pain — on the model of action that feminists assume — would, for such a woman,

---

[3] This is what Firestone misses when she says 'machines may soon equal or surpass man in original thinking and problem-solving' (*The Dialectic of Sex*, p. 190).

constitute 'liberation' from the ordeal and offer a means of obtaining relief. Through this, it is suggested, she would feel once more in control of the situation. The other woman, victim of equally brutal suffering, staunchly resists any interference by anaesthetists in the sensations of birth.[4] Imagine that she receives positive encouragement from those attending her — perhaps her mother and the father of her child, even the midwife — to accept the pain in full consciousness. Now, according to Beauvoir's account, such an attitude can make sense only if the woman is a masochist and if those encouraging her are anti-feminist.[5]

In short, then, the contrast between the two women can be expressed as follows: the first woman raises herself beyond a merely animal level through the technological control exercised over her pains, while the second woman fails precisely because she submits to the forces of nature. Yet this actually contradicts what we would normally say in the situations in question.

Significantly, the woman who readily accepts an anaesthetic — despite the technical assistance she may have at her disposal — by that very act relinquishes her capacity for action and reduces herself to a passive thing. Sometimes this is due to the effects of the particular medication, for, as Sheila Kitzinger warns:

We may accept medication for pain relief . . . as necessary in childbirth and not recognize its disadvantages. In the case of Pethidine these are many. It sends women into a drowsy stupor in which labour can take on

---

[4] The need for such behaviour has, of course, to be understood within the context of a modern hospital, where childbirth has become 'technologized'. See, for example, Kitzinger, *Women as Mothers*, chapter 6, 'Ritual and Technology in Contemporary Hospital Childbirth', for a more ample description of the sort of situation I am imagining.

[5] some anti-feminists are indignant in the name of nature and the Bible at any proposal to eliminate labour pains, which they regard as one of the sources of the maternal 'instinct'. Helene Deutsch seems somewhat drawn to this view. . . . This . . . evidently stems from the fact that she regards woman as doomed to masochism, her thesis compelling her to assign a high value to feminine suffering. (Beauvoir, *The Second Sex*, pp. 485 – 6n.)

a nightmare quality, reducing the ability to cope with pain, and making it impossible to control breathing and relaxation. (*Women as Mothers*, p. 159)

Kitzinger is drawing attention to the fact that with this sort of pain relief the very act of eliminating pain inevitably brings with it a loss of active control. Of course, this result should hardly strike us as surprising if we accept, as indeed Simone de Beauvoir exhorts us to do, that the human being is not composed of two substances — body and mind — contingently connected but that to be a human being is to be embodied. We must understand, therefore, that we cannot blot out physical sensations without also blotting out consciousness of, and perhaps control over, the events we are experiencing (the degree to which this occurs will depend on the nature of the anaesthetic). Thus someone who has a general anaesthetic before a surgical operation necessarily accepts that just as he will be oblivious of the pain, so will he play no active role during the operation and will have no conscious memory of the events surrounding it. In short, loss of control and consciousness is not just a possible side-effect of pain relief; it is inevitable. Hence the incoherence of Beauvoir's claim that anaesthetization of birth necessarily makes a woman an active agent, even where the sense of agency is limited to control over natural events.

It is because of the disadvantages of much medication for pain relief that regional anaesthetics, of which the most well-known is the lumbar epidural, have been hailed as the answer to pain in childbirth. An epidural certainly can allow for pain-free, even sensation-free labour without impairing the general consciousness of the woman. In fact, obstetricians boast that with the advantages of epidural anaesthesia, patients can read or watch television while their baby is being born.[6] However — and this question is crucial to our discussion here — do the effects of this sort of anaesthetic show that a woman has more conscious control, is more active, is more of an agent *vis-à-vis* her procreative functions? The short answer to

[6] See Kitzinger, *Women as Mothers*, p. 161.

this is no. An epidural, particularly when it is administered successfully, numbs the lower abdomen and legs, usually down to the feet. Hence, while the woman may well be 'free' to read during the birth of her baby, as far as the actual birth process is concerned, she is a mere passive spectator. The complete lack of sensation, which leaves her oblivious of the contractions occurring in the uterus, takes away her urge to push the baby out of the vagina, thereby utilizing those uterine contractions to facilitate and expedite the delivery of the infant. This means that the obstetrician is obliged — precisely because the mother, her sensations being dead, cannot actively participate in the birth of the child — to take over, to usurp, the natural role of woman during childbirth as *he* now 'gives birth' to the baby with the aid of an array of technological devices which include forceps, foetal monitors and catheters.

Some writers are inclined to see the behaviour of the obstetrician in such circumstances as unjustifiable. For instance, Kitzinger describes his role in modern hospital childbirth as follows: 'The obstetrician, as distinct from the midwife who is traditionally far less interventionist, *seeks* to take control of childbirth. It is then almost as if he, and not the woman, gives birth to the baby.' (ibid., p. 154; my italics) But this distorts the facts of the situation which, as I have aimed to point out, are such that the woman cannot save herself the pain of childbirth without at the same time relinquishing conscious control over the event.

This point is also missed by Anne Oakley in 'Wisewoman and Medicine Man'. According to her, the depersonalization and horrors of the 'hospitalized and increasingly technological pattern of childbirth management' (p. 53) reveal 'one common denominator: the insistence that the modern *male-controlled* system has a tendency to treat women not as whole, responsible people but as passive objects for surgical and general medical manipulation' (p. 54; my italics). At the same time, she laments the delayed use of anaesthesia in midwifery at the beginning of the century, when it had 'obvious relevance' (!) (p. 34), which she attributes to the general anti-woman attitude of the medical profession. Like Kitzinger, however, she fails to realize that the effect of *technology*-controlled childbirth

— whether this is supervised by male or female obstetricians — is that active women, potentially fully conscious of their painful birth pangs, are inevitably transformed into objects of inert flesh precisely in order that a 'solution' to the labour pains may be found.[7]

Consequently, the real choice facing women who wish to have conscious, active control over their labour and the birth of their children is not whether to have a male obstetrician or a female midwife, but whether or not to accept anaesthetics. (Of course, this is not to say that there may not be other good reasons why obstetrics should be exclusive to women.)

Incidentally, it is for reasons of this sort that such charities as the National Childbirth Trust in this country have made it their business to protect women and their babies from technology in childbirth. And, given that feminists like Firestone agitate for the rights of women to be agents, it is extraordinary that natural childbirth should be regarded by them as 'only one more part of the reactionary, hippie-Rousseauean, Return-to-Nature' rejection of the desirability of total control of human life by technology (*The Dialectic of Sex*, p. 189). Yet they are inevitably drawn to this conclusion, given their conception of action.

Firestone thinks that a woman undergoing natural childbirth is pretending to experience 'a real trip, some mystical orgasm (that faraway look)' (p. 189). What is being sought, she seems to imagine, is a kind of 'intuitive' oneness with nature, the implication of which, as we saw in the discussion on Simmel and intuitive knowledge in chapter 3, is that woman is passive. Nothing could be further from the truth, however. For, as Danaë Brook points out in *Naturebirth*, a preparatory text for natural childbirth,

accepting the truth is intrinsic to this preparation. By this I mean that painting pretty pictures doesn't help us deal with harsh reality. To delude is not to prepare. Giving birth is one of the most extraordinary experiences of life. It can be wildly uncomfortable while it lasts. It can

---

[7] Cf. Marx's observation: 'The machine accommodates itself to man's weakness, in order to turn *weak* man into a machine.' (*Early Writings*, p. 360).

be desperately painful. But one's understanding of and response to pain can change. I believe we can control the degree to which the action of the womb during labour affects us. I don't think that any of it, either the preparation or the experience itself, is easy. I have found that nothing that is rewarding in life is easy. The truth and reality of birth is that for most people natural labour is hard work which demands hard practice beforehand. (p. 134)

Now, it is precisely because the behaviour of our second hypothetical woman in labour cannot be called mere passivity that notions like practice, work and control have such a central role to play in Danaë Brook's attempt to distinguish 'naturebirth' clearly from the sort of approach Firestone considers typical of natural labour advocates. A useful way in which to explore some of the distinctive features of natural labour, as opposed to 'artificial' labour, might be to begin with the contrasts in the physical aspects of the two situations, what Georg von Wright calls the 'immediate outer aspect' of forbearance.

In cases of action which can be described as intentional passivity von Wright observes, as we noted on p. 131f, that the outer aspect of such action consists 'exceptionally, [in] muscular activity which one "lets go on" although one could restrain the movements'. This is a very precise description of what is required by a woman seeking control during natural labour. Essentially, natural childbirth preparation teaches the woman 'a relaxation technique which helps you go to the point where . . . you do not fight involuntary muscle tension with more tension' (Brook, *Naturebirth*, p. 131). And because the most immediate and natural reaction of a person to involuntary muscle tension — for a woman in labour, such tension is manifest in contractions — is voluntarily to tense up other muscles in the body, a tremendous effort is required by a woman in labour to resist this temptation. This involves above all her consent to let the contractions go on without fighting them: 'The physical exercises teach you how one set of muscles can be at work while the rest of the body stays loose and easy.' (p. 134) In short, the effort involved is an effort to remain passive. And again: 'the most important thing to remember about transition. . . . is that you need to breathe in a way that *stops* you from doing exactly what you feel like doing.' (p. 208) All this is achieved through conscious, controlled breathing, which is why Brook warns against the use of analgesics: 'Contractions don't stop if you take painkillers; but your ability to control, or take an active part in your labour, is inevitably hampered.' (p. 129)

So far, then, the point is that the behaviour appropriate in relation to the involuntary contractions of labour is 'intentional passivity' or 'inactive action'.[8] However, during the actual birth the entire emphasis changes to 'productive' action. This is because an enormous positive effort (as opposed to the negative effort[9] necessary during labour), consisting of great physical strength and concentration, is required of the woman as *she* pushes the baby out of the vagina with the combined force of the uterine contractions and her voluntary bearing-down efforts. Fully conscious of the sensations she is experiencing, she participates in the birth, with her baby, by 'reinforcing the natural expulsion of the baby from the uterus by being aware enough to utilize contractions for pushing' (p. 211). It is at this point that the inhibiting effects of pain-killing medication

---

[8] This description of 'intentional passivity' as 'inactive action' comes from Simone Weil: 'Good is essentially other than evil. Evil is multifarious and fragmentary, good is one, evil is apparent, good is mysterious; evil consists in action, good in non-action, in activity which does not act, etc. . . .' (*Gravity and Grace*. p. 63) Goodness consists also in 'Detachment from the fruits of action. To escape from inevitability of this kind. How? To act not *for* an object but *from* necessity. I cannot do otherwise. It is not an action but a sort of passivity. Inactive action.' (ibid., p. 39)

[9] Most often attention is confused with a kind of muscular effort. If one says to one's pupils: 'Now you must pay attention', one sees them contracting their brows, holding their breath, stiffening their muscles. If after two minutes they are asked what they have been paying attention to, they cannot reply. They have been concentrating on nothing. They have not been paving attention. They have been contracting their muscles. . . . Attention is an effort, the greatest of all efforts perhaps, but it is a negative effort. (Weil, *Waiting on God*, pp. 70−1}

Interestingly, an important way of helping women in labour passively to attend to their contractions is to make them conscious of the symptoms of their failure to do this. On such occasions, women are nearly always 'contracting their brows, holding their breath, stiffening their muscles'.

are likely to turn the situation into what Kitzinger, for instance, describes as a 'nightmare'. The situation is analogous to that of a drunk trying to drive carefully on a busy highway. Conversely, at this point a woman giving birth naturally is likely to describe the experience as a potent, exhilarating and creative act; think of Anna's experience of labour in *The Rainbow* (quoted on p. 31 above).

Simone de Beauvoir says that a woman cannot assign a high value to suffering unless she is a masochist (*The Second Sex,* p. 485n.); Firestone simply asserts that pregnancy is barbaric and that since childbirth hurts, it is bad for women (*The Dialectic of Sex,* pp. 188—9); other women, as we have already seen on p. 32 above, simply cannot understand where the deep significance of childbirth is supposed to lie — 'I just don't want to know anything about it. I think all that stuff about the joy of birth is a lot of nonsense.' The claim seems to be that a woman can accept suffering only if she is a subservient and passive creature or if she is mad. This is false. Hence our difficulty here is to elucidate the aims or cognitions present in the wider context of birth that make it intelligible for a woman to reject pain-killers without necessarily relinquishing her right or desire to be an agent. Many possible accounts can be given, for as we have already noted, conventions are never strictly determined by natural facts. The following account I offer should therefore be taken as *one* such example.

The way things go for us in our lives is not something that is totally under our control. For even the rational, liberated feminist in Firestone's Utopia, who does not die of old age,[10] may be struck by lightning. And even if ours is a society which can pride itself on having developed painless dying, we may still be victims of a war or of a natural disaster, in which the death we have to face may be a

---

[10] Full mastery of the reproductive process is in sight, and there has been significant advance in understanding the basic life and death process. The nature of ageing and growth, sleep and hibernation, the chemical functioning of the brain and the development of consciousness and memory are all beginning to be understood in their entirety. This acceleration promises to continue for another century, or however long it takes to achieve the goal of Empiricism: total understanding of the laws of nature.'(Firestone, *The Dialectic of Sex,* p. 170)

bitter, painful, desolate affair, alleviated neither by the support and sympathy of others nor by pain-killing medication. For those who predicate the peculiar distinctness of human life on mankind's ability to be master over nature, such distasteful facts may lead some of us to the conclusion that human life is, after all, a paltry affair, mere animal existence. However, to others it may mean that the human condition is such that with life, we must accept death; with joy, we must accept woe; with pleasure, we must accept suffering. It may be argued that this is what it means to be human and embodied: 'For everything there is a season, and a time for every matter under heaven: a time to be born, and a time to die. . . .' (*Ecclesiastes* 3: 1—8) It may suggest that technological independence from suffering (say) is only a spurious form of independence, and that ultimately 'There is only one man who gets his own way — he who can get it single-handed; therefore freedom, not power, is the greatest good' (Rousseau, *Emile*, p. 48).

From this point of view, a woman may regard it as a form of escapism or idealism to imagine that pain-killing drugs can solve the problem of pain for her. And even if we consider only the physical conditions of artificial childbirth that I have described above, she would be justified in thinking this. For she may reject the view, seen by many as thoroughgoing realism, that the 'cognitive and technical superiority' of our scientific, industrial way of life is 'so manifest, and so loaded with implications for the satisfaction of human wants and needs — and, for better or worse, for power — that it simply cannot be questioned' (Gellner, 'The New Idealism', p. 155). Indeed, she may argue that since this assumption *can* be questioned, Gellner may, in fact, be closer to idealism than those he criticizes. It is questioned every day by women who go through the horrors of giving birth in labour wards which look like 'scientific hell-holes with instruments everywhere, wires everywhere' (S. Simmons, 'Induction of Labour', p. 14) and who find that whereas 'the traditional mode of childbirth places the woman in the centre of the unfolding drama, modern childbirth involves advanced and sophisticated technology and cumbersome equipment compared with which the labouring woman seems dwarfed and insignificant' (Kitzinger, *Women as Mothers*, p. 151).

Moreover, she may regard physical suffering as an inexorable fact of the human condition and, further, as a vital element in the creation of the new life in which she plays a part and may therefore humbly accept her suffering. She may regard such suffering as so fundamental to her conception of the nature of life, of the conditions necessary for its creation, that she would regard it as a failure to dull the pains in any way.[11] Her feeling might be that to want the baby without the pains would be cheating. To adopt some means of avoiding the suffering would be to betray something that matters to her and to violate her moral sense of the significance of the natural order:

> Nothing begins, and nothing ends,
>> That is not paid with moan,
> For we are born in other's pain,
>> And perish in our own.
>
> (Thompson, 'Daisy')

Consequently, childbirth is not experienced as an isolated event. The sense it has for her depends on the unity that she is able to see between her various activities, interests and relations with others. This may show itself in the fact that her relations with her mother are founded on feelings of gratitude and responsibility, special and distinct from those she may feel towards her father. Perhaps it shows itself too in the fact that she tends to think of herself, in relation to her child, not as a property owner but as a vehicle through which the child has entered the world:

And a woman who held a babe against her bosom said,
Speak to us of Children.

---

[11] This view is naturally subject to the labour's being normal and without complications.

And he said:
Your children are not your children.
They are the sons and daughters of Life's longing for itself.
They come through you but not from you,
And though they are with you yet they belong not to you.

You may give them your love but not your thoughts,
For they have their own thoughts.
You may house their bodies but not their souls,
For their souls dwell in the house of to-morrow, which you
cannot visit, not even in your dreams.
You may strive to be like them, but seek not to make them
like you.
For life goes not backward nor tarries with yesterday.
You are the bows from which your children as living arrows
are sent forth.
The Archer sees the mark upon the path of the infinite, and
He bends you with His might that His arrows may go swift
and far.
Let your bending in the Archer's hand be for gladness;
For even as He loves the arrow that flies, so He loves also
the bow that is stable.
(Gibran, *The Prophet*, pp. 20−3)[12]

And so on.

Schaffer thinks that technological developments show that the biological facts of birth are not sacrosanct (see above, p. 125). This seems plausible only because he misses the point that biological facts occur within a *human* context and that what is sacrosanct, therefore, are the human thoughts, values and traditions enveloping the facts

---

[12] Firestone says: 'A mother who undergoes a nine-month pregnancy is likely to feel that the product of all that pain and discomfort "belongs" to her ("To think of what I went through to have you!").' (*The Dialectic of Sex*, p. 216) But where Gibran encourages unselfish love on the part of the mother, Firestone stipulates that natural pregnancy and birth should be destroyed in favour of artificial reproduction, so that the possibility of such maternal possessiveness cannot even arise. Disastrously, she fails to see that this destruction eliminates the possibility not only of possessiveness but also of love.

of birth. This means that the restrictions that some people may feel compelled to impose on certain types of interference in the birth process — for example, contraception — may derive not initially or fundamentally from a lack of manipulatory know-how but from moral constraints which are absolute and final. Says Sheila Kitzinger:

When I was in South Africa a Zulu chief who is also a senior witchdoctor explained to me the ceremony of 'stopping the wombs of the women'. The use of contraception was a political, not a personal decision. The Elders met and discussed the situation, and *before further action could be taken had to offer sacrifices and prayers seeking forgiveness of the ancestors.* Small pebbles were then collected from a special sacred river and in the ceremony one was slipped into the uterus of each woman of child-bearing age. (*Women as Mothers,* p. 80; my italics)

Thus the onus on anyone who wishes to argue as Schaffer does must be to show that a *moral* constraint can be old-fashioned, pre-scientific and barbaric. . . .[13] Consequently, despite the opportunities technological developments may provide for interference in these vital processes, our freedom to exercise such rights indiscriminately may, in many circumstances, be an illusory one. All this brings us back to the point that the notions of agency and manipulative action are not synonymous.

Feminists may find intolerable the thought that suffering in childbirth is something we need to learn to accept. Still, they have not shown — and this point is crucial to their arguments — that unless a woman has full manipulatory control over her reproductive functions, her right to be an agent is violated. Ironically, to the extent that it can be shown that interference during labour and birth, for instance, actually impairs a woman's agency, feminists give every reason why the right to such interference is a demand that should be struck from their manifestos. However, this outcome is unlikely, given their conception of agency and action.

[13] See Peter Winch, 'Understanding a Primitive Society' (reprinted in *Ethics and Action*), for a full treatment of this point.

Feminists claim, then, that since women are 'enslaved' by their reproductive functions, liberation for them necessarily involves technical control over these functions. To deny them such control is, in effect, to deny them their agency. I repeat, therefore, a point made earlier, that the issues surrounding birth control revolve around the feminist conception of action. This point is emphasized, albeit not in the philosophical terms I am using, in an incisive discussion by Lucinda Cisler of the importance of birth control for feminism. She points out that much general discussion of abortion reveals a failure to come to terms with the significance of this from a feminist perspective:

Repeal is based on the quaint idea of *justice*: that abortion is a woman's right and that no one can veto her decision and compel her to bear a child against her will. All the excellent supporting reasons — improved health, lower birth and death rates, freer medical practice, the separation of church and state, happier families, sexual privacy, lower welfare expenditures — are only embroidery on the basic fabric: *woman's right to limit her own reproduction*.

It is *this* rationale that the new woman's movement has done so much to bring to the fore. Those who caution us to play down the woman's-rights argument are only trying to put off the inevitable day when society must face and eradicate the misogynistic roots of the present situation. And anyone who has spoken publicly about abortion from the feminist point of view knows all too well that it is *feminism* — not abortion — that is the really disturbing idea. ('Unfinished Business', p. 309)

According to a feminist view of action, once it is admitted that women deserve the right to be free and equal — to be agents, in short — there can be no logical argument against birth control. Feminist argument in favour of birth control has gone uncontested for the most part — except, of course, by the Roman Catholic Church. It might be interesting, therefore, to consider whether the prevalent view that the Roman Catholic Church's teaching on birth control serves to oppress women is justified.

Feminists point out that among the various religions the Roman

Catholic Church is singled out for criticism because 'by its stand against birth control and abortion, and by its skilful and wealthy lobbies to prevent legislation change . . . [it] presumes to rule on the lives and bodies of millions of women' (Morgan, *Sisterhood is Powerful*, pp. xxi—xxii). In so doing, it condemns women to a life of passivity. Feminists say this, even though they are prepared to admit that the Pill may have serious side-effects, detrimental to the health of women and that other forms of contraception may not be very effective, because although 'Technology is not God, and will not provide salvation . . . if one of its most highly touted products [the Pill] isn't available, settling for second- or third-best is still preferable to passivity' (Cisler, 'Unfinished Business', p. 282). This means that the crucial question that the Roman Catholic Church is required to answer by feminists is whether it can be shown that the prohibition of birth control does not violate the rights of women to be agents.

It is important to remember that the Roman Catholic Church does in fact sanction birth control. It stipulates, however, that such control is permissible only through the use of natural methods. Leaving aside the special theological arguments that it advances to sanction natural birth control as opposed to control that depends on the use of artificial contraceptives — these are irrelevant to the feminist debate — our difficulty is to see whether the Roman Catholic Church is justified, on feminist grounds, in according special status to natural birth control.

The ovulation method of natural birth control, sanctioned by the Roman Catholic Church, is a method by which a fertile woman can be taught to recognize the fertile days of her cycle by observing a vaginal discharge which indicates fertility.[14] The method can be summarized thus:

It pays attention to the cervical mucus which is the critical factor in conception. The development of the mucus tells a woman . . . there is

---

[14] For full details of this method, see Billings, *The Ovulation Method of Natural Family Planning*. Incidentally, this method is reported to be more 'efficient' than the rhythm method, which Billings describes as obsolete.

now present in her body a secretion which may nourish the sperm cells and keep them in a healthy state even for a few days awaiting ovulation. The practical rule, therefore, is quite obvious: all sexual contact must be avoided on those days when the mucus is present. (Billings, *The Ovulation Method of Natural Family Planning*, pp. 8–9)

Natural birth control differs from artificial contraceptive methods in that the efficiency of the former method depends wholly on the voluntary self-control that a couple is able to exercise over desire. Failure in this respect constitutes a failure in the method.

Now, if the feminist argument in favour of artificial contraception, as we saw above, turns on the thought that through it women distinguish themselves from animals by not being 'abandoned wholly to nature' (Beauvoir, *The Second Sex*, p. 467), it is difficult to see why Roman Catholic insistence on natural birth control should be thought to restrict the control that women are able to exercise over their lives. Indeed, if it is at all intelligible to say that 'the reproductive function . . . has come under the voluntary control of human beings' (ibid.), it would seem that the Roman Catholic approach is the one which most encourages women to exercise voluntary control over their reproductive functions. It is an odd notion to suggest that someone who uses a device, in the form of a pill or whatever, to prevent something from happening is exercising voluntary control over his or her bodily functions. A man who claimed to be fasting but was found to be relying on appetite depressants at the same time would be considered a cheat. Moreover, if one of the crucial points in the feminist argument is that women gain freedom (to some extent, at any rate) from their 'oppression' through the use of contraceptives, it would seem that Roman Catholic insistence on natural methods has much to commend it to a feminist. A woman who is able to distinguish *for herself* the occasions on which she is fertile is independent of the good will of drug companies, which may or may not continue to manufacture contraceptives, and of the 'benevolence' of patriarchy in permitting the distribution of contraceptives, despite their supposed threat to the sexist *status quo*. In addition, it means that the exercise of the restraint necessary for this form of birth control rests squarely on the shoulders of both the man and the woman. If conception is not desired, they must both assume full responsibility for avoiding it by sexual abstinence. The man can no longer indulge in 'bourgeois bad faith' by shirking responsibility and by leaving the problem of contraceptive measures to the woman, who in any case (for obvious reasons) cannot be expected to accept sole culpability and responsibility should those measures prove to be inefficient.

Nevertheless, this does mean — and this is a fact that feminists are loth to admit — that a fundamental feature of the sexual act is that it may result in conception. Feminists insist that women have the right to be agents. This is quite right. But it means that in so far as coition is an act between two people *qua* responsible agents — human life is never abandoned wholly to nature (Beauvoir) — and in so far as the sexual act *is* potentially a procreative act, the responsibility of a man and a woman for conception that is the result of their sexual union is theirs to accept and to acknowledge, whether they failed to abstain during the critical period when using the ovulation method or because the contraceptive devices they used failed.

Feminists believe that it is sexually responsible to make sure that one is using some form of contraception if a pregnancy is not desired. Hence they contend that if all reasonable precautions are taken against pregnancy, abortion may be regarded as a legitimate way out if a woman still becomes pregnant. This argument will not do. From the Roman Catholic point of view, the real point is that sexual responsibility means accepting the fact that the sexual act is, fundamentally and potentially, a procreative one. People who do not wish to accept this fact and the responsibility it entails should not have sex.[15] The same applies to those who, because of their emotional

---

[15] Nevertheless, despite the Church's perhaps justified distrust of and aversion to artificial birth control, its popular presentation of the issues involved tends to be inconsistent.

The Encyclical Letter of Pope Paul VI, *On Human Life*, begins by acknowledging man's 'stupendous progress in the domination and rational organization of the forces of nature to the point that he is endeavouring to extend this control over every aspect

immaturity or their economic dependence on others (to mention only two possible reasons) — for example, juveniles — would not be able to honour such obligations even if they wanted to. And it is precisely because the marriage ceremony involves the couple's formal consent to accept children (a point strenuously emphasized by the Roman Catholic Church) — which is another way of saying that they publicly and formally accept that the sexual act is potentially a procreative one — that the proper place of sex is considered to be inside marriage rather than outside it. That is why a married woman — that is, a woman who has formally accepted the potential relation that exists between sex and procreation — who gave up her child for adoption or had an abortion would be judged more severely than an unmarried girl who did the same thing.

The upshot of this is that the feminist desire to deny the natural relation which exists potentially between sex and procreation is neither simply a revolt against the so-called authoritarianism of the Roman Catholic Church nor a revolt against so-called sexist, patriarchal convention; it is also a revolt against nature. This point

---

of his own life — over his body, over his mind and emotions, over his social life, and even over the laws that regulate the transmission of life' (p. 6). If an essential point in the argument against artificial contraception, therefore, is that we must accept that 'there are certain limits, beyond which it is wrong to go, to the power of man over his own body and its natural functions — limits, let it be said, which no one, whether as a private individual or as a public authority, can lawfully exceed' (p. 18), and that the Church urges man 'not to betray his personal responsibilities by putting all his faith in technical expedients' (p. 19), then surely the question of artificial birth control is but one issue among many in the modern world with which Roman Catholics ought to be engaged in continuous and total confrontation. That they are not tends, on the one hand, to encourage a vulgar identification of morality with sexual morality on the part of many Roman Catholics and, on the other hand, to suggest that the Church seems ready to tolerate the use of certain technical expedients which are decidedly immoral as long as they are unconnected with sexuality. It is a source of confusion to some Roman Catholics that the Church does not speak out as strongly against, for example, weapons capable of mass destruction and that many Roman Catholics unashamedly see nothing immoral in these.

At any rate, it is a pity that this whole area of birth control, which merits serious discussion and thought, is considered to be related peculiarly to the Natural Law and therefore to be of no relevance to those who do not subscribe to such a doctrine.

emerges quite explicitly from the following assertion by Juliet Mitchell:

> Reproduction [and] sexuality . . . need to be free from coercive forms of unification. . . . The revolutionary demand should be for the liberation of these functions from an oppressive monolithic fusion. This dissociation of reproduction from sexuality frees sexuality from alienation in unwanted reproduction (and fear of it), and reproduction from subjugation to chance and uncontrollable causality. It is thus an elementary demand to press for free state provision for oral contraceptives. The straightforward abolton of illegitimacy as a legal notion as in Sweden and Russia has a similar implication; it would separate marriage civicly from parenthood. (*Woman's Estate*, p. 150)

That this is all sophistry should be particularly apparent in the light of what I have already said regarding the feminist view that nature, and not patriarchy, is the oppressor of women.

Hence, even from a secular point of view, the distinction between contraception and abortion is an important one. Lucinda Cisler is therefore quite wrong to say:

> Although it is always sad when people are afraid to give things the right names, whether something 'is' contraception or abortion is actually of little consequence in evaluating the result; the goal is the prevention of an unwanted birth, and whatever will achieve this aim safely and surely we can simply call 'birth control' and be done with it. ('Unfinished Business', p. 299)

A crucial difference between someone who relies on a contraceptive to prevent a birth and someone who relies either on abortion or on abortifacients — for example, the intra-uterine device and the hoped-for 'morning-after' pill — is that the latter explicitly rejects and defiles the natural relation that exists between sex and procreation. It does not necessarily follow, therefore, as many feminists seem to think, that if contraceptives are legally admissible then the same automatically follows for abortions. If it does, then it is difficult to see why the natural progression from abortion should not be to infanticide.

Feminists criticize our society — justly — for being one in which the rationale of the economic system is based on waste and destruction. They resent the exploitation of women by the agents of capital:

We know that the so-called sexual revolution was only another new form of oppression for women. The invention of the Pill made millions for the drug companies, made guinea pigs of us, and made us all the more 'available' as sexual objects; if a woman didn't want to go to bed with a man now, she must be hung-up. (Morgan, *Sisterhood is Powerful*, p. xxv)

And so it might seem that the ovulation method, which is in no danger of making millions for anyone (neither the drug companies nor the Roman Catholic Church) and which costs nothing, by contrast with the costly use of resources and energy expended in the production of artificial contraceptives, could, from a feminist point of view, be an acceptable alternative to conventional birth-control practices.

Yet, for all this, a position like the Roman Catholic one must fall flat on its face because notions like agency, freedom and voluntary control are linked in the minds of feminists — and generally in the intellectual atmosphere of our times — with a conception of action in which one-sided emphasis is laid on 'productive' action. Action which is intentional passivity, therefore, is seen only as an expression of mere passivity and impotence. Because the emphasis is so much on doing as opposed to refraining, on acting as opposed to contemplating,[16] feminists seem capable of recognizing behaviour as action only if some practical difference is made to the world.

[16] Cf. what T. S. Eliot, for example, has to say about this:

> The endless cycle of idea and action,
> Endless invention, endless experiment,
> Brings knowledge of motion, but not of stillness;
> Knowledge of speech, but not of silence;

Incidentally, this is the reason, too, why feminists think the traditional emphasis on feminine virtues such as obedience, humility and patience only encourages women to give in to their oppression. This may be true, but whether such a claim is valid will depend on the circumstances. For it is important to remember that obedience is not the same as subservience; humility is not the same as masochism; and patience is not the same as impotence. The distinction can be expressed by saying that the first category presupposes agency and the second aims to destroy it, so that (for example) obedience differs from subservience by being a case of intentional passivity as opposed to mere passivity. Thus even though a feminist may reject the view that patience is the 'correct' attitude to take to suffering, it cannot be argued that a woman who so responds must be an unwitting victim of oppression. And if the general feminist claim is that justice demands that women are to be respected as persons and as agents — which is how I think most people think of feminism — then it follows that much feminist declamation is unjustified.

Knowledge of words, and ignorance of the Word.
All our knowledge brings us nearer to our ignorance,
All our ignorance brings us nearer to death,
But nearness to death no nearer to God.
Where is the Life we have lost in living?
Where is the wisdom we have lost in knowledge?
Where is the knowledge we have lost in information?
The cycles of Heaven in twenty centuries
Bring us farther from God and nearer to the Dust.
(Chorus 1 from 'The Rock', in *Collected Poems 1909–1962.*)

7

Concluding Remarks

In discussing writers like Firestone and Beauvoir, I tried to show that feminists fully recognize that the biological differences between the sexes form the axis around which justification for, and discussion of, differential treatment of the sexes must turn, which is why they stipulate that a feminist revolution is bound to be impeded while the differences between the sexes remain inviolate. And my suggestion there was that their motivation for rejecting the reality of sex differences seemed to originate from a revolt against nature and against the human condition, rather than from a desire to implement social changes which would embrace more fully, and with more justice, such differences and their consequences for women.

It is worth noting that this revolt against the human condition is not peculiar to feminism but is a striking feature of our times. Hannah Arendt, for instance, draws attention to this modern phenomenon by attaching the following significance to the event many saw as a victory for man: his landing on the moon. She remarks:

although Christians have spoken of the earth as a vale of tears and philosophers have looked upon their body as a prison of mind or soul, nobody in the history of mankind has ever conceived of the earth as a prison for men's bodies or shown such eagerness to go literally from here to the moon. Should the emancipation and secularization of the modern age, which began with a turning-away, not necessarily from God, but from a god who was the Father of men in heaven, end with an even more fateful repudiation of an Earth who was the Mother of all living creatures under the sky?

The earth is the very quintessence of the human condition, and earthly nature, for all we know, may be unique in the universe in providing human beings with a habitat in which they can move and breathe without effort and without artifice. The human artifice of the world separates human existence from all mere animal environment, *but life itself is outside this artificial world, and through life man remains related to all other living organisms.* For some time now, a great many scientific endeavors have been directed toward making life also 'artificial', toward cutting the last tie through which even man belongs among the children of nature. It is the same desire to escape from imprisonment to the earth that is manifest in the attempt to create life in the test tube, in the desire to mix 'frozen germ plasm from people of demonstrated ability under the microscope to produce superior human beings' and 'to alter [their] size, shape and function'; and the wish to escape the human condition, I suspect, also underlies the hope to extend man's life-span beyond the hundred-year limit. (*The Human Condition*, pp. 2—3; my italics)

To the many endeavours that have been directed, according to Arendt, towards making life 'artificial' may be added the feminist endeavour to construct, among other things, an androgynous world, a world in which sex differences are absent. It is significant that Arendt implicates the rebellion against human existence with the attempt to separate human existence totally from all mere animal life. This is related to the point that feminists reject the domestic role of women because they think that only those activities for which there is absolutely no parallel in the animal world are distinctly human (see chapter 1). Hence the feminist response is entirely in keeping with the unquestioned axiom of an age in which either no significance is attached to, or a deliberate attempt is made to ignore, the fact that 'through life man remains related to all other living organisms'. Feminists are trying to escape from the fact that woman will always be related to animal life because she is indissolubly linked with the life process through, among other things, her reproductive role. (Men, too, of course, are related to animal life.) Caught in the falsehoods of the rationalist net, they are therefore compelled to deny, and even to destroy, life — the demand for abortion is the most articulate expression of this — in order to feel both equal with men and distinct from animals. That the liberation of women is to be grounded in this death-wish is a grotesque irony; it cannot but be disastrous for both women and society.

This irony is particularly disturbing because a genuine sexual revolution — the liberation of women from sexist (puritanical) attitudes to sexuality and to femininity — would be based on a celebration of *life*: a celebration of the sensuous, passionate, pulsating, vibrant life that pours forth between two lovers in sexual union *and* a celebration of the life that may burst forth and flourish should the man's seed be fertilized by the woman. Yet feminists encourage us to regard conception as an aberration, which ought to be eliminated from sex, and to regard the fact that human beings are sexual beings — that one is either a *man* or a *woman* — as a curse upon humankind. But in wanting to destroy sex distinctions, feminists poison sexuality itself — they abstract it and divorce it from the physical, flesh-and-blood, *male* and *female* human beings in which it manifests itself immediately and naturally. It exists only as an Idea. In a feminist Utopia sex is hypostatized into a phantom power, which sexless beings pursue but in vain. Devoid of vital male and female human beings, it is a world of abstract beings seeking abstract pleasures.

In his *Early Writings* Marx criticizes Hegel for positing the movement of history on abstract, speculative thought instead of on man. Hegel's starting-point is abstract self-consciousness; Marx's starting-point is man:

Man is directly a *natural being*. As a natural being and as a living natural being he is on the one hand equipped with *natural powers*, with *vital powers*, he is an *active* natural being. . . . On the other hand, as a natural, corporeal, sensuous, objective being he is a *suffering*, conditioned and limited being, like animals and plants. . . . man is a *corporeal*, living, real, sensuous, objective being with natural powers. . . . To be sensuous is to *suffer*. . . .

Man as an objective sensuous being is therefore a *suffering* being, because he feels his suffering [*Leiden*], he is a passionate [*leidenschaftliches*] being. (ibid., pp. 389—90; Marx's italics)

Therefore, it seems to follow, a being who does not suffer is a non-sensuous, non-objective being. And 'a non-objective being is a non-being' (ibid). One implication of Marx's argument seems to be that man cannot escape from suffering without at the same time alienating himself from his natural, corporeal being. He cannot escape from it unless he regards himself as an abstract self-consciousness, a non-being. It would seem, then, that man is doomed to suffer precisely because, as a flesh-and-blood, sensuous being, he is subject, as are all other living organisms, to the contingencies of life. To look forward, as feminists do, to a time when the problems of living will be 'solved' is symptomatic of alienation from nature, of self-estrangement.

Curiously, however, the whole animus of Marx's work — and of our age — rejects this conclusion. He insists that communism is the

genuine resolution of the conflict between man and nature, and between man and man, the true resolution of the conflict between existence and being, between objectification and self-affirmation, between freedom and necessity, between individual and species. It is the solution of the riddle of history. . . . (ibid., p. 348)

And with this Marx involves himself in a contradiction. He forgets, or fails to see, that the very notion of a 'movement of history' towards some prescribed goal, that extravagantly abstract and idealistic conception on which the whole Hegelian edifice ultimately rests, is itself a sophistry which cannot, at the same time, acknowledge that man *is* a natural being whose life is therefore always subject to certain limits and conditions. This is because recognition that man is a corporeal, flesh-and-blood, sensuous, natural being means acknowledging also that he must remain steadfastly bound, through all time, to facts that know no movement and do not change: birth, suffering, death, the conflict between freedom and necessity and so on. Consequently, it throws into jeopardy the very idea of a progressive movement or a *dialectic* of history, thereby showing that Marx's conception of a communist state — a state in which the conflict between man and nature is supposed to be resolved — is itself a symptom of the alienation from nature which he criticized in Hegel. Even as a mere theoretical construct, the notion of a communist state — the solution of the 'riddle of history' (?), the resolution of the conflict between freedom and necessity, etc. — depends for its plausibility not so much on the abolition of private property as on the total estrangement of man from his human *nature*. Neither the socialization of the means of production nor the Hegelian dialectic can transform the natural conditions of human existence without substituting for the living, natural, passionate, human being a soulless, artificial hybrid. Communism aims, among other things, to promise the resolution of conflicts which, as Marx himself seems at times to have realized, are at the heart of human existence. But this is nothing less than the empty, speculative promise of the Hegelian dialectic. A really critical approach to the Hegelian system would therefore recoil not only from idealism, but also from talk of dialectics.

The inveterate belief in progress and in a dialectic of history goes hand in hand with an abstract conception of human life. It is a belief that reveals the alienation of men from nature, and, since man is a natural being, it is symptomatic of self-estrangement. Nevertheless, it is no accident that a feminist Utopia must be a world in which birth, sex and death no longer exist. This notion of a dialectic of history — or, to use Firestone's expression, a dialectic of sex — depends for its credibility on the artificial construction of human life as something *un*conditioned and *un*limited. But we cannot destroy the limited and conditioned aspect of human life without necessarily destroying that part of ourselves through which we remain related to nature and to all other living organisms: life itself.

Bibliography

Annas, Julia 'Plato's *Republic* and Feminism', *Philosophy* 51, 1976

Annas, Julia 'Mill and the Subjection of Women', *Philosophy* 52, 1977

Arendt, Hannah 'The Crisis in Education', in *Between Past and Future: Eight Exercises in Political Thought* (New York: Viking Press, 1958)

Arendt, Hannah *The Human Condition* (Chicago: University of Chicago Press, 1974)

Aristotle *The Politics*, translated by T. A. Sinclair (Harmondsworth: Penguin, 1964)

Beauvoir, Simone de *The Second Sex*, translated by H. M. Parshley (London: Jonathan Cape, 1953)

Beels, Christine *The Childbirth Book* (London: Turnstone Books, 1978)

Billings, John *The Ovulation Method of Natural Family Planning* (compiled by Ovulation Method Advisory Service, PO Box 33, Brian Boru Street, Cork)

Bowlby, John *Maternal Care and Mental Health* (Geneva: World Health Organization, 1951)

Brook, Danaë *Naturebirth: Preparing for Natural Birth in an Age of Technology* (London: Heinemann, 1976)

Cisler, Linda 'Unfinished Business: Birth Control and Women's Liberation', in Robin Morgan (ed.), *Sisterhood is Powerful* (New York: Vintage, 1970)

Cohen, Gerry 'Belief and Roles' *Proceedings of the Aristotelian Society, 1966—1967, 67*

Dostoyevsky, F.M. *Crime and Punishment*, translated by David Magarshack (Harmondsworth: Penguin, 1976)

Durkheim, Emile *The Rules of Sociological Method*, translated by Sarah A. Soloray and John H. Muelles (New York: Free Press, 1964)

Eliot, T. S. 'Choruses from "The Rock"', in *Collected Poems 1909—1962* (London: Faber and Faber, 1972)

Encyclical Letter of Pope Paul VI *Humanae Vitae (On Human Life)*, translated by Alan C. Clark and Geoffrey Crawford (London: Catholic Truth Society, 1970)

Firestone, Shulamith *The Dialectic of Sex: The Case for Feminist Revolution* (London: Women's Press, 1979)

Fisher, Mark 'Reason, Emotion and Love', *Inquiry* 20, 2—3, 1977

Freud, Sigmund *The Standard Edition of the Complete Psychological Works of Sigmund Freud*, ed. J. Strachey, Vols 1—24 (London: Hogarth Press/Institute of Psychoanalysis, 1959)

Gellner, Ernest 'The New Idealism', in Anthony Giddens (ed.), *Positivism and Sociology* (London: Heinemann, 1974)

Gerth, H. H., and Mills, C. Wright (eds.) *From Max Weber* (London: Routledge and Kegan Paul, 1977)

Gibran, Kahlil *The Prophet* (London: Heinemann, 1970)

Gladwin, T. 'Cultural and Logical Process', in N. Keddie (ed.), *Tinker, Tailor . . . The Myth of Cultural Deprivation* (Harmondsworth: Penguin, 1976)

Gordon, Linda 'Functions of the Family', in Leslie B. Tanner (ed.), *Voices from Women's Liberation* (New York: Signet Books, 1970)

Gould, Carol 'The Woman Question: Philosophy of Liberation and the Liberation of Philosophy', in Carol C. Gould and Marx W. Wartofsky (eds.) *Women and Philosophy* (New York: Putnam, 1976)

Hardy, Thomas *The Woodlanders* (London: Macmillan, 1973)

Hegel, Georg *Philosophy of Right*, translated by T. M. Knox (New York: Oxford University Press, 1973)

Hegel, Georg *Logic*, translated by William Wallace, *The Logic of Hegel* (Oxford: Clarendon Press, 1874)

Jeffers, Robinson 'Poetry and Survival', *New York Times Magazine*, 18 January 1953

Jones, J. R. 'How do I know who I am?' *Proceedings of the Aristotelian Society*, supplementary volume, 1968, 42

Kant, Immanuel *Groundwork of the Metaphysic of Morals*, translated by H. J. Paton, in *The Moral Law* (London: Hutchinson, 1969)

Keddie, Nell (ed.) *Tinker, Tailor . . . The Myth of Cultural Deprivation* (Harmondsworth: Penguin, 1976)

Kierkegaard, Soren *Purity of Heart* (New York: Harper Torchbooks, 1956)

Kitzinger, Sheila *Women as Mothers* (London: Fontana, 1978)

Kuhn, Thomas *The Structure of Scientific Revolutions* (Chicago: University of Chicago Press, 1971)

Lawrence, D. H. *The Rainbow* (Harmondsworth: Penguin, 1969)

Leon, Philip *The Ethics of Power, or the Problem of Evil* (London: Allen and Unwin, 1935)

Marx, Karl *Early Writings*, translated by Rodney Livingstone and Gregor Benton (Harmondsworth: Penguin/New Left Review, 1975)

Marx, Karl, and Engels, Friedrich 'Manifesto of the Communist Party', in Lewis S. Feuer (ed.), *Marx and Engels: Basic Writings on Politics and Philosophy* (London: Fontana, 1969)

Mead, Margaret *Male and Female* (Harmondsworth: Penguin, 1976)

Melden, A. I. *Rights and Persons* (Oxford: Basil Blackwell, 1977)

Millett, Kate *Sexual Politics* (London: Granada, 1972)

Mitchell, Juliet *Woman's Estate* (Harmondsworth: Penguin, 1971)

Mitchell, Juliet 'Women and Equality', in Mitchell and Oakley, *The Rights and Wrongs of Women* (Harmondsworth: Penguin, 1977)

Mitchell, Juliet, and Oakley, Ann *The Rights and Wrongs of Women* (Harmondsworth: Penguin, 1977)

Morgan, Robin (ed.) *Sisterhood is Powerful* (New York: Random House, 1970)

Morris, Jan *Conundrum* (Falmouth: Coronet, 1975)

Muggeridge, Malcolm *Something Beautiful for God* (London: Collins/Fount, 1980)

Myrdal, Gunnar *The Political Element in the Development of Economic Theory* (London: Routledge and Kegan Paul, 1953)

Natanson, Maurice *The Journeying Self: A Study in Philosophy and Social Role* (Reading, Mass.: Addison-Wesley, 1970)

Newson, John, and Newson, Elizabeth *Patterns of Infant Care in an Urban Community* (Harmondsworth: Penguin, 1966)

Oakley, Ann 'Wisewoman and Medicine Man: Changes in the

Management of Childbirth', in Mitchell and Oakley, *The Rights and Wrongs of Women* (Harmondsworth: Penguin, 1977)

Phillips, D. Z., and Mounce, H. O. *Moral Practices* (New York: Schocken, 1970)

Plato *The Republic*, translated by A. D. Lindsay (London: Dent, 1937)

Rhees, Rush *Without Answers* (London: Routledge and Kegan Paul, 1969)

Rhees, Rush 'The Tree of Nebuchadnezzar', in *The Human World*, no. 4, 1971

Rhees, Rush 'Mario und der Zauberer', in *The Human World*, no. 6, 1972

Riesman, David *The Lonely Crowd* (Yale: Yale University Press, 1969)

Rousseau, Jean-Jacques *Emile*, translated by Barbara Foxley (London: Dent, 1977)

Rowbotham, Sheila *Woman's Consciousness, Man's World* (Harmondsworth: Penguin, 1977)

Sartre, Jean-Paul *Being and Nothingness*, translated by Hazel Barnes (New York: Washington Square Press, 1971)

Schaffer, Rudolph *Mothering* (London, Fontana/Open Books, 1977)

Schopenhauer, Arthur *On the Basis of Morality* (Indianapolis: Bobbs-Merrill, 1965)

Shainess, Natalie 'A Psychiatrist's View: Images of Woman — Past and Present, Overt and Obscured', in Robin Morgan (ed.), *Sisterhood is Powerful* (New York: Vintage, 1970)

Sherfey, Mary Jane 'On the Nature of Female Sexuality', in Jean Baker Miller (ed.), *Psychoanalysis and Women* (Harmondsworth: Penguin, 1974)

Simmel, Georg 'Das Relative und das Absolute im Geschlechter-Problem', in *Philosophische Kultur* (Leipzig: Kröner, 1919)

Simmons, S. 'Induction of Labour', *Proceedings of the Third Study Group of the Royal College of Obstetricians and Gynaecologists*, 1975

Spock, Benjamin *Baby and Child Care* (London: W. H. Allen, 1979)

Spock, Benjamin *Raising Children in a Difficult Time* (London: New English Library, 1974)

Sturt, George *The Wheelwright's Shop* (Cambridge: Cambridge University Press, 1976)

Thompson, Francis 'Daisy', in *An Anthology of Modern Verse*, chosen by A. Methuen (London: Methuen, 1953)

Tolstoy, Leo *The Kreutzer Sonata and Other Tales*, translated by Aylmer Maude (London: Oxford University Press, 1973)

Tolstoy, Leo *Anna Karenin*, translated by Rosemary Edmonds (Harmondsworth: Penguin, 1977)

Wallace, William (trs.) *The Logic of Hegel* (Oxford: Clarendon Press, 1874)

Weil, Simone 'Human Personality', in *Selected Essays 1934—1943* chosen and translated by Richard Rees (London: Oxford University Press, 1962)

Weil, Simone *First and Last Notebooks* (Oxford: Oxford University Press, 1970)

Weil, Simone *Gravity and Grace,* translated by Emma Craufurd (London: Routledge and Kegan Paul, 1972)

Weil, Simone *Oppression and Liberty*, translated by Arthur Wills and John Petrie (London: Routledge and Kegan Paul, 1972)

Weil, Simone *Waiting on God*, translated by Emma Craufurd (London: Fountain Books, 1977)

Weil, Simone *The Need for Roots*, translated by A. F. Wills (London: Routledge and Kegan Paul, 1978)

Weininger, Otto *Sex and Character* (London: Heinemann, 1906)

Weston, Michael *Morality and the Self* (Oxford: Basil Blackwell, 1975)

Winch, Peter 'Authority', *Proceedings of the Aristotelian Society*, supplementary volume, 1958

Winch, Peter *Ethics and Action* (London: Routledge and Kegan Paul, 1972)

Winch, Peter *The Idea of a Social Science and its Relation to Philosophy* (London: Routledge and Kegan Paul, 1972)

Wittgenstein, Ludwig *Zettel*, translated by G. E. M. Anscombe (Oxford: Basil Blackwell, 1967)

Wittgenstein, Ludwig *Philosophical Investigations*, translated by G. E. M. Anscombe (Oxford: Basil Blackwell, 1974)

Wittgenstein, Ludwig *The Blue and Brown Books* (Oxford: Basil Blackwell, 1975)

Wittgenstein, Ludwig *Remarks on the Foundations of Mathematics* (Oxford: Basil Blackwell, 1978)

Wollstonecraft, Mary *A Vindication of the Rights of Women* (Harmondsworth: Penguin, 1978)

Wright, Georg von *Explanation and Understanding* (London: Routledge and Kegan Paul, 1971)

Index